AMA Complete Guide to
SMALL BUSINESS MARKETING

Kenneth J. Cook

AMERICAN
MARKETING
ASSOCIATION

NTC Business Books
a division of *NTC Publishing Group* • Lincolnwood, Illinois USA

Library of Congress Cataloging-in-Publication Data

Cook, Kenneth J. (Kenneth Joseph)
    AMA guide to small business marketing / Kenneth J. Cook.
        p.   cm.
    Includes bibliographical references and index.
    ISBN 0-8442-3590-3
    1. Marketing—Management. 2. Small business—United States—
-Management. I. Title
HF5415. 1.C595   1992
    658.8—dc20   92-18353
                                                                            CIP

Published in conjunction with the American Marketing Association,
250 South Wacker Drive, Chicago, Illinois, 60606.

1994 Printing

Published by NTC Business Books, a division of NTC Publishing Group.
© 1993 Kenneth J. Cook

3 4 5 6 7 8 9 BC 9 8 7 6 5 4 3 2

Foreword

Ken Cook and I have talked frequently about the perils of small business management, the challenges of increasing regulation, and, significantly, the need for capital. A recurrent theme in our conversations was our belief that good commercial bankers truly wanted to help small businesses grow and prosper. Reality, however, dictated that small businesses could not attract the attention of the commercial bankers unless their stories were compellingly told.

Ken and I agreed that a good marketing plan was as helpful as any information in a company's "story." Not only can a banker learn about the business, its focus, and its projects from a marketing plan, but also about the ability of the owner to organize thoughts, communicate them effectively, and design good control measures.

The same techniques that he recommends for his readers—keep it simple, show "how-to" in a straightforward and easily readable presentation—are what Ken used to craft this book. The liberal use of white space, bullets, short paragraphs, and good editing help to accomplish his objectives. Sticking to this format makes it easy for the reader to move through the book. One technique that sets Ken's approach apart is the use of understandable worksheets that guide the reader in the formulation of a marketing plan. Too many of the how-to books are so highly conceptual that the reader never benefits from concrete advice. The reader can simply build on these worksheets to write the plan in stages.

Small businesses are often managed in short bursts while satisfying customer needs, counseling with associates, and attending to demanding administrative tasks. Ken has designed a program that allows the small business person to put the book aside and return to the right place so that he or she can build a workable and presentable marketing plan.

Entrepreneurs, their bankers, and investors all will benefit from a well-written business plan. Ken Cook's guide is a new and useful tool in business planning.

Robert C. Sammons
Vice President
Founders National Trust Bank

Contents

Step Three: Rating Target Markets 58

Step Four: Developing Sales Plans 74

Afterword 106

Appendix 109

Worksheets 121

Index 158

Acknowledgments

This program would not have been possible without the contribution of my advisors. Their support and critical input was invaluable. My thanks to:

Robert Cook Sr.—Because of his years of experience in sales and marketing, he was able to remind me of the cardinal rule: *Keep it simple!*

Jeff Klank—His experience working with smaller businesses helped me shape content to their needs.

Roger Vacca—A business owner with common sense and a practical outlook. He helped me apply that to this work.

Lew VanAntwerp—Lew made concrete contributions to the program with his constructive input and excellent analysis techniques. My thanks to him for sometimes keeping my thinking straight.

Anne Knudsen and Karen Shaw—Anne and Karen believed in my project and saw the potential benefits it offered. As my editors, they championed my work and helped bring it to fruition.

A special thanks to my wife, Candis Cook. She applied a critical eye to everything I did. Her desire to "make this program the best it can be" is, in my opinion, reflected in the outcome. The content and logic of the program reflect some of her excellent thinking.

She believed in what I was trying to do, and supported my efforts 100 percent. I appreciate her patience, her faith, and her assistance in helping make my goals attainable.

Finally, thanks to my clients. I have learned from each one of them.

Introduction

Let's talk about a small business. According to the U.S. Department of Commerce and the Small Business Administration, approximately 80 percent of all independently owned small businesses will fail within the first three years. As a small business owner or executive, you work hard to avoid becoming a statistic. Being effective in your efforts depends, to some degree, on understanding why some businesses fail and some do not. Let's explore some of the issues that impact success or failure.

Small Business Is Vulnerable

Small businesses, by definition, are not large. They do not have the resources to tackle whole industries or markets. They can not afford many mistakes. Mistakes cost money; lost money negatively affects cash flow; cash flow is the life blood of a small business. Consequently, a small business owner needs to be very precise in his/her strategic thinking. Precise thinking will lead to fewer mistakes. Fewer mistakes should help your cash flow. A strong cash flow reduces vulnerability.

Small Business Is Quick

Nature has given every species on the planet some proprietary defenses. The large are often slow, and the small are often fast. In the business world, a defense available to small businesses is their speed; their ability to adapt quickly to changing situations and customer needs. This is necessary for survival. To remain quick, the business owner must be knowledgeable and focused. Without knowledge and focus, speed could be a detriment because the direction chosen might be wrong.

Small Business Is Entrepreneurial

An entrepreneur is one who organizes and manages an enterprise, and assumes the associated risk. There are three key words in that definition—organizes, manages, and risk. Being an entrepreneur is neither good nor bad. It is a frame of mind. The successful entrepreneur is one who knows how to organize, how to manage, and how to reduce risk.

Small Business Can Become Big Business

Almost every large corporation started small. They became big because someone had a vision of what they could be and was determined to make it happen. Making that vision reality required execution.

Small Business Runs Differently from Big Business

Big corporations have many resources, many staff people. Small business guards it resources, surviving with little or no staff. As a result, small businesses have to do some things differently—especially marketing. Big businesses have resources for market research activities and sophisticated customer measurements. Not having these tools available means that small businesses must be resourceful. They must find other, less expensive ways to gain the same kind of customer information.

The successful and profitable small business owners or executives incorporate many of the above themes and characteristics. They are:

- Precise thinkers
- Knowledgeable
- Focused
- Organized
- Good managers
- Calculated risk takers
- Visionaries
- Good planners
- Good listeners
- Resourceful
- Results oriented

The planning process you are about to embark on will not instill in you all of the above traits. What it will do is help you understand how to apply these traits in the context of your marketing and sales efforts.

You know there are customers out there who can use your products and services. This program will help you identify and capture them.

Marketing in the Small Business Environment

If you are a small business owner, one of the key issues you consider is balancing your time. The problem, of course, is that you have too much to do and never enough time to get it all done. The other side of this is that the tasks required of small business vary widely— inventory, accounting, personnel, recruitment, organization, sales, marketing, and payroll. Being human, we emphasize what we do best; we spend most of our time doing the things we like. But, being business people, we know we need to balance our preferred activities with those "got-to-do" activities.

Some people like marketing, some do not. Whether you like marketing is not the issue. You *need* marketing to achieve balance in your business.

Just what is marketing? Is it sales? No. Tom Bonoma of Harvard Business School writes the best definition I have seen: "Marketing is the function through which the firm encourages exchanges of goods for money that are profitable to it and satisfying to its customers."[1] Good marketing can generate activities that help you pursue the most profitable, highest volume sales possible, in the context of your resources.

You can't avoid marketing. Any contact with customers is marketing. The issue is one of marketing *quality*. How much time do you spend considering the quality of your marketing? This is important.

This program is all about your company and its marketing. It will take about 40–50 hours for you to complete this program. I know that for some of you I need to rationalize dedicating that much of your time to market planning. Here it is: If you complete this program properly, you will end up with a marketing plan that will appreciably enhance your ability to grow your business, and to grow it profitably. Maybe even more important, it will help you understand *why* you had success, so you can repeat it over and over. Does this sound like a good use of your time? Together, we are going to develop a marketing plan for your business. Done properly, it will be realistic, able to be implemented, measurable, and profitable!

I know you have heard a lot about marketing plans. They are everywhere. The only one that matters is yours. You know there are customers out there who can use your products and services. This program will help you identify and capture them.

Why bother with a marketing plan? Obviously, you already have a lot of expertise or you would not have your own business. Obviously, you are doing some marketing, or you would not have any customers. Here's why: *Planning impacts success.* A major computer industry distributor and franchisor did a study to find out what factors made their franchisees fail or succeed. The result is interesting. Their analysis showed a single key element that separated the winners from the losers. That element was planning. The successful franchises had a plan. The failed franchises did not plan. It was the existence of a plan and the business owner's commitment to execute that plan that foretold success.

This program is a plan development process. The content of the program reflects some of the top marketing thinking of the decade. The work necessary to complete the program will be done by you. In essence, the program is a marketing consultant you have on board without incurring the associated thousands of dollars of expense.

The program is an innovative approach for giving a small business owner the knowledge and focus necessary to be successful in the marketing and sales game. This design and approach can help you conserve your cash flow and profits.

How the Program Works

This is a plan development process. It will help you determine the critical data required for successful marketing and sales. If implemented properly, it will help you get orders and reorders.

The program contains four steps:

1. Selecting target markets

2. Analyzing target markets

3. Rating target markets

4. Developing sales plans

Each step builds upon the data gathered in the previous step. The text explains the concepts you will apply to your business. Following the explanations, there are Action Points you will need to complete. Included are worksheets for completing these assignments. The worksheets will step you through a logical approach to making solid marketing choices.

The worksheets are grouped into packets. There is a foundation packet (**Worksheets A–D**) that applies in all the target markets. You will also need one additional packet for each target market you analyze (**Worksheets 1–13**).

This may seem like a lot of worksheets. Recognize that you do them one at a time—with a logical flow from one to another. When completed, the worksheets themselves comprise your comprehensive marketing plan for each target segment.

The sample sheets contain information about a real company and a real marketing and sales situation they faced. The company is a distributor in the truck after-market. They do about $2 million annually in sales. The issue they faced was how to gain a greater market share of the clutch business with customers who had large fleets of trucks.

Let's preview the contents of each step in the program and their corresponding worksheets.

Step One

Step One, Selecting Target Markets, is a screening process. You cannot be everything to everyone. A profitable business focuses its efforts on customers it has a good chance of getting. In section one, you are going to begin the process of identifying your good customers. You will segment your market and learn about the customers in each segment. You will find out the who, what, when, where, why, and how of them. You will then weed out unattractive segments and select potential target markets. This step uses Worksheets 1, 2, 2A, and 3.

Step Two

Step Two, Analyzing Target Markets, is the data gathering portion of the program. You identified target markets in Step One. Now, you will gather data on yourself and your competition. The data will form the base for making strategic marketing and sales decisions. In this step, you will use Worksheets 3–7 and A–D.

Step Three

Step Three, Rating Target Markets, is an evaluation system. Based on the data collected from Step Two, you will rate each target market. You will test your ability to satisfy the customer's needs and beat the competition. The ratings will show which target markets offer the highest potential. Step Three uses Worksheets 2–9.

Step Four

Step Four, Developing Sales Plans, is like writing a road map. The sales program is the blueprint of actions and tactics you will use to get orders and reorders. We will look at advertising, publicity, sales promotions, and personal selling. We will examine when to use each tactic. We will look at feedback mechanisms and why they are so important. When this step is complete, you will know what sales steps to take to reach the customers you target. You will use Worksheets 10–13 for this final step.

A Note about External Forces

External forces are situations or occurrences outside of your company's control. Small business can be vulnerable to these. There are many external forces to consider:

- Government regulations
- New state or federal laws
- Plant closings/plant openings
- Major businesses moving into or out of an area
- Government facilities opening or closing
- New technologies introduced in the market
- Activities of key suppliers

This program focuses on things that you can research, that are in your control. It does not focus on the external forces of the marketplace. You know your business environment. Please factor external forces into your marketing plan judgments.

AMA Complete Guide to
SMALL
BUSINESS
MARKETING

Selecting Target Markets

Developing a marketing and sales plan can help increase revenues and profits. This process begins by selecting target markets. In this step, you will reduce the universe of potential customers into a manageable group of target markets. Selecting target markets involves a series of screening decisions. This decision process is not precise, nor should it be. The process is realistic. You have limited time and limited financial and personnel resources to conduct research, so you need to apply your resources in such a way that you gain maximum benefit with minimum expenditure. This screening process helps you do that.

Step One has four parts:

1. Target marketing
2. Segmenting your market
3. Profiling your customers
4. Qualifying your market segments

Target Marketing

Target marketing is a focused, planned approach for identifying and winning the customers whose needs you can best satisfy. Target marketing gives you a competitive edge by helping you identify better marketing opportunities. Target marketing helps you leverage your resources so that instead of spreading resources thin trying to attract any customer you can focus resources on customers whom you can satisfy. This saves you money and increases the return on your marketing dollars.

Your goal is to win a market. You are looking for a niche where some aspect of your company, products, or services will allow you to dominate. You want to define a target market where you are the leader—where you set the standards. You should want to own that market.[2]

Segmenting Your Market

A *market segment* is a group of customers related by some common characteristic(s). These customers may have common needs, require similar products, buy for similar reasons, or operate in similar manners. Some segments may be profitable. Others may be breaking even, and there may be some that are losing money. Your goal is to apply resources and sell only in segments where you can make revenues and profits.

The question is: What market segments offer solid revenue and profit potential? The answer is: Any market segment where you satisfy the needs of the customer offers the potential for solid revenues and profits. This is a simple answer. Notice that the focus is on the customer. You need to identify specific market segments where you can satisfy needs.

To get to this point, you need to know what market segments exist. Identifying market segments can be done in many ways. Following are some of the techniques available to segment your market. Please take some time to reflect on these concepts.

Vertical Industries

A *vertical industry* is a group of customers related by the business they are in, and is often a natural starting point for segmenting. Automotive, retail, or real estate are examples of vertical industries. A vertical industry in this form, however, is still too large to be valuable in your segmenting effort. You need to identify subsets of the industry.

The common characteristic used to segment a vertical industry is the needs of the customers. Consider the following examples.

Retail

Retailers come in many forms. There are department stores, convenience stores, food and drug stores, and specialized retailers (apparel, audio/video, carpet, etc.). They all have different needs.

A common need of specialized retailers is attractive furniture and fixtures for display of merchandise. Because of this need, specialized retail stores could become a market segment for

1. Interior design firms
2. Interior decorators
3. Companies that make display cases
4. Furniture stores
5. Carpet stores

Automotive

Like retailers, automotive companies take many forms. There are new car dealers, used car dealers, leasing companies, parts suppliers, and repair and service companies.

Effective inventory management is a need for parts suppliers. Because of this need, automotive parts suppliers could become a market segment for

1. Software vendors
2. Computer hardware companies
3. Accounting firms
4. Systems consultants

The following are more examples of businesses and the market segments they may find in vertical industries.

1. Meat wholesalers: Market segments include restaurants, food distributors, cafeterias, grocery stores, and butcher shops.
2. Medical supply companies: Market segments include hospitals, doctors' offices, dentists' offices, clinics, and nursing homes.
3. Plumbing contractors: Market segments include general contractors, multiple-location businesses, home builders, and construction firms.

Buying Patterns

A second technique for segmenting markets is identifying *buying patterns*. Customer needs shape buying patterns. Needs dictate how often customers buy. Needs dictate the amount a customer buys per purchase. Needs determine when a customer buys.

You can segment your market based on the buying patterns of customers. You may choose to serve only customers who are low-volume buyers. You may choose the opposite—only high-volume buyers. You may choose to set a minimum buying volume that customers must spend with you. You may choose to set a maximum buying volume.

For example, companies that have fleets of automobiles buy many cars. They often replace cars when they reach a preset number of miles. These buying patterns of high volume and replacement, regardless of condition, may make companies with fleets a market segment for automobile dealers. The dealers could be new car dealers who want to sell cars or used car dealers who want to buy the fleet of cars to be replaced.

General contractors often buy large volumes of building materials. The high-volume buying pattern may make general contractors a market segment for lumber yards, cement companies, and hardware supply companies.

Point of Purchase

Another segmenting technique is determining *point of purchase*—where and how customers buy. Catalogs, dealers, storefronts, and salespeople are examples of the point of purchase. (You might also think of this as your *channel of distribution*, that is, the channel through which you reach your customer.)

The point of purchase identifies a need on the part of the customer. Catalog customers may want convenience. Customers who buy in a store may need to see and compare products. Customers who buy through salespeople may need information before they decide.

For example, customers who buy personal computers need technical information. Because of this, salespeople dominate computer sales. These salespeople are knowledgeable and can provide the information the customer requires. The point of purchase—salespeople—satisfies the customer need for information.

Most customers who buy pizza want speed and convenience, not an elaborate sit-down dinner. So, pizza firms offer fast service in the restaurant, or by delivery. The points of purchase—in the restaurant or at-home delivery—satisfy the customer need for speed and convenience.

The secret to using this technique is matching the needs of your customer with the appropriate point of purchase. For segmenting purposes, the point of purchase will lead you to customers who make up a market segment. The common element in the segment is the need associated with the point of purchase—convenience, information, etc.

Product Mix

Identifying *product mix* at time of purchase is another segmenting technique. Product mix is the array of products a company offers and the way those products are combined to meet the needs of customers.

Start-up businesses, for example, need a lot of basic materials. This market segment can be targeted by a printer offering a mix of products including business cards, stationery, envelopes, and invoices. The product mix satisfies the need for simplicity and serves the market segment.

Businesses without in-house accountants may still need help with taxes, payroll, auditing, and some business/management consulting. They may be an excellent market segment for the accounting firm to pursue. An accounting firm can offer a broad product mix including preparation of tax information and returns, payroll management, auditing, and consulting services. This product mix allows the firm to satisfy the needs of businesses that cannot or do not wish to do the accounting work internally.

Information Requirements

Satisfying information requirements is another segmenting technique. You recognize that a certain segment of the market will require training with your product. You offer that training. The group of customers requiring training becomes a market segment. This type of segmenting technique is especially effective with new technologies or new complex products.

A good example is a small video retailer who sells camcorders. The owner recognizes that a percentage of customers need training to operate the camcorders. As a service, he offers training. Large department stores may not offer the training. The small retailer will outsell a large department store with the group of customers who require training. The information requirements of the customer creates a segment where the small retailer can win.

Geography

A sixth technique is geographic segmentation. You sell to firms within a specific city, state, region, or nation. Usually, you use a geographic definition of segments in combination with some other method of segmenting your markets.

Summary of Techniques

Here is a summary of some of the most common variables for segmenting markets. These are partial lists. You may discover other variables more pertinent to your business. If so, use them. You may combine variables to form segments as well. Use the techniques that make sense for *your* business.

The lists are broken into two distinct groups—consumer market variables and commercial market variables. Review the lists and consider which of the variables will be most appropriate for segmenting your markets.

Major Segmentation Variables for Consumer Markets[3]

- **Geographic:** Local, state, region, national, international.
- **Demographic:** Age, sex, marital status, family size, income, occupation, education level, religion, race, nationality.
- **Psychographic:** Social class, life-style.

Major Segmentation Variables for Commercial Markets[4]

- **Demographic:** Industry, company size, company location.
- **Operating Variables:** Usage (light, medium, or heavy), purchasing criteria (quality, service, price).

As you research your market segment(s), you will begin to learn about your potential customers. Bear in mind the following:

1. All segments are not the same size
2. Customers can be in more than one segment
3. One segment can be a subset of another
4. A segment can stand alone and be unique within the market
5. The size of the segment is not important in itself; what counts is the revenue potential

Look at the following graphic. The outer circle encompasses the universe of potential customers. That universe breaks down into groups of customers that share some characteristic(s). Those groups of customers are market segments represented by the smaller circles.

How Existing Businesses Segment Customers

Whether you are an existing or start-up business affects the approach you take in segmenting your universe of potential customers. If you are an existing business, you have a good data base of information to work with—your current customers. You need to look at your customers to see how common characteristics can segment them into groups.

- Are they in the same type of business or industry?
- Do they have the same needs?
- Is there a commonality in the point of purchase?
- Do they buy for the same reason(s)?
- Do they buy the same product mix?
- Do they require information to make a decision?

You also need to look beyond current customers for expansion considerations. Use the information from your current customers as a base point. Expand your thinking about the needs and the commonalities that exist. Look for potential customer groups who have those same needs or characteristics. The information sources discussed for start-up businesses may be helpful to you in this process.

How Start-up Businesses Segment Customers

If you are a start-up business, there is additional work you will need to do. You do not have an existing base of customers as a starting point. You need to research the industry to determine who the typical customer is for your products and services. There are several resources you can use to gather information.

1. A good source of data is an industry association. Most industries have an association that tracks the trends, facts, and figures about the industry. Contact this type of association to see what information it can provide.

2. Your future competitors are a good source of information. Determine who their customers are, and you should know

who your customers are. Of course, your future competitors probably will not offer such information. Some "intelligence gathering" is needed. If you are opening a retail store, visit competitors' stores. Observe the customers and see what you can learn. Follow competitors' delivery or service trucks. See who they visit. Become a customer of your competitor. Ask questions. You will be surprised what you can learn.

3. If you are opening a franchise, the franchisor should provide standard information. The detail may be limited, but it should be an excellent starting point.

4. Marketing research firms do extensive investigation into a wide spectrum of industries. This resource has an expense associated with it. Investigate the research firm and be sure their research methodology and quality of data will give you what you need.

5. Speciality consultants also do research. Like the research firms, there is an expense associated with the service. The same caution mentioned with market research firms applies here.

6. Trade journals and publications about the market segments you are considering can provide information. The local library should have a copy of the Gale Directories. These books contain listings of all periodicals printed in the United States. Use them to see what magazines you should review.

7. Trade shows can provide a wealth of information. The periodicals or the industry association should have information about the dates and locations of trade shows. Walk around the show. Ask questions. Take copies of the scores of free material available. Read the materials. Talk to other attendees. The attendees are your potential customers.

8. Your own experience will also help. Most people are familiar with the industry in which they start a business. If you have some familiarity with your industry, you have some knowledge about the typical customer. Apply that knowledge to help you identify market segments.

9. Another source is the local college or university. Business school professors sometimes look for market research projects their students can do. Your research needs may be just the project they are looking for.

The appendix at the end of this book contains a list of companies and publications that provide market data.

 ## *Action Point*

Your first assignment is to apply the market segmentation techniques to your business and identify the market segments that exist.

Write the name and description of each market segment you identify on **Worksheet 1.** Remember to use a separate Target Market Packet of worksheets for each market segment. ■

Profiling Your Customers

At this point, you should have a fairly long list of different market segments. Now it is time to make the list manageable.

The first thing to do is to get to know your customers by identifying their needs, benefits sought, and purchasing characteristics. Do not assume you know this information. Define it from the customer's perspective.

Before you start, review the following definitions.

- Customer needs: A *customer need* is a desire, goal, or objective the customer wants to attain. A need relates to the customer's business. For example, contractors might need improved job cost control. Manufacturers might need reduced down time. A need for a homeowner might be a maintenance free home exterior. The need is something the customer wants to accomplish as it relates to business or home life.

- Customer benefits sought: A *benefit sought* is the result a customer wants to achieve through satisfying a need. Again, it is from the customer's perspective. Improved job cost control for the contractor means a reduction of material and labor costs and possibly increased profits. Reduced down time for a manufacturer means higher production rates and potentially higher revenues. A maintenance-free home exterior means more time for family and leisure activities. All these examples indicate what the customers expect in the form of benefits if their needs are satisfied.

- Purchase characteristics: *Purchase characteristics* are the behaviors and requirements associated with your customers' buying habits. For example, you want to know where they purchase your types of products and services. You want to know the volume of purchases they make in a specific time frame. You want to know their price expectations.

The only way to learn about customer needs, benefits sought, and purchase characteristics is to *ask the customers.* For existing businesses, "customers" means not only your current customers, but also the potential customers you are targeting. You must understand the customers' needs before you can select target markets. Asking the customer can be done several ways. The variables to address are who to ask, what to ask, and how to ask.

Who to Ask

The members of the market segments you identified represent who to ask. Contact customers or potential customers in each segment. You should interview as many customers as possible. The customers chosen should represent a cross section of the customers in the segment. You are looking for a base of information that shows the needs, benefits sought, and purchase characteristics of your market segment.

What to Ask

There are three tools you will use to help you determine what to ask—the **Critical Linkages Analysis,** the **Critical Impacts Analysis,** and the **Purchase Characteristics Questionnaire.** All three tools apply in business-to-business research. If you are researching consumer market segments, the **Critical Impact Analysis** does not apply.

Critical Linkages Analysis

The first tool looks at critical linkages.[5] A linkage is a connection point, a point of contact between your customer and you. *Critical linkages* are the connection points that really count—they define your relationship with your customer.

Your customers probably come into contact with you in many areas. Typical among them are sales, service, order entry, inventory, engineering, and administration. Of course, these vary according to the type of business.

Regardless, your goal is to determine what in your organization is important to your customers. You need to ask them to rank linkages with you. You need them to tell you, from their perspective, what connection points are critical.

Where they define a connection as critical, customers are expressing a need or associated benefit. You need to know if a customer believes that the link to a part of your company is critical to doing business with you. As importantly, you want to understand *why* the customer perceives this link as critical. (Critical linkages offer an excellent opportunity for differentiation—something we will discuss later.)

To help you understand what linkages are critical, and why they are critical, you will conduct a critical linkages analysis with customers in each market segment. Look at the **Critical Linkages Analysis** diagram at the end of this step. This is the tool you will use to learn your customers' critical links. There are three types of diagrams. In the upper left hand corner of each one is a code. "D" is for distribution; if you are a distribution company, use this sheet. "M" is for manufacturing; if you are a manufacturing company, use this sheet. "S" is for service providers; if you are a service company, use this sheet. Use only the diagram for your type of company.

Now have your customer depict critical linkages. One circle says "Suppliers to _____ ." Fill your company's name in the blank. Notice that each form has some blank circles so that you can modify them to resemble more closely the structure of your organization. Modified or not, take one of your **Critical Linkages Analysis** forms to each member of your target market that you survey. Ask the customer to draw lines connecting it to the parts of your organization where contact is important. After drawing the lines, have the customer rank the lines in sequence of importance. The example at the end of this step shows a completed diagram.

Once your customer has completed the analysis form with lines and rankings, ask him or her to explain why the top three links are critical. Ask *why* the customer rated them the top three. How do they impact the customer's ability to do business with you? Answers to these questions will show what needs the customer has in the context of your organization. Use the **Critical Linkages Analysis** pages 2–3 to prompt your questions and record the customer's responses. (Pages 2–3 are the same in each critical linkages form—S, D, or M.)

Critical Impacts Analysis

The second tool is the **Critical Impacts Analysis.**[6] Here, you want to determine how your products or services impact the customer's business. The tool works similarly to the **Critical Linkages Analysis,** except in this case you want the customer to show how your products or services impact the customer, rather than how he or she links to your company.

For example, if you are a supplier to a manufacturing company, your ability to deliver as promised impacts your customer's production scheduling. This may have a ripple effect on the company's ability to deliver to its customers and the resultant level of customer satisfaction. You need to know these impacts that are present in the seller/buyer relationship between you and your customers.

There are three forms for the **Critical Impacts Analysis.** Use form "M" if your customer is a manufacturer, form "S" if your customer is a service provider, and form "D" if your customer is a distributor. In the center circle, fill in the name of your product or service. As before, ask the customer to draw lines to show impact. In this case, the customer draws lines from your product or service, (depicted in the center of the page) to various parts of his company. The lines show where your products and services are critical to the customer's operation—from the *customer's* perspective.

After drawing the lines, have the customer rank the top three lines in sequence of importance. Where the customer shows a critical impact, they are expressing benefits sought in the context of your products and services. Understanding these benefits sought is essential to developing a strong relationship with your customer. Like the **Critical Linkages Analysis,** the **Critical Impacts Analysis** has three pages. The questions on the last two pages will help you explore the underlying benefits sought associated with the top three critical impacts.

Purchase Characteristics Questionnaire

The third tool is a **Purchase Characteristics Questionnaire.** Use one of the two questionnaires in the Appendix, depending upon your company. If your company sells products, use the products questionnaire. If your company is a service provider, use the services questionnaire.

The **Purchase Characteristics Questionnaire** contains core questions for you to use to assess purchase behavior. The questions explore points of purchase, key purchase criteria, purchasing plans, pre- and post-service requirements, etc. Use these questions, modify them, or add more for your situation, as appropriate. Consider customizing the questions for your company and situation. The more specific and precise you can be, the more accurate your feedback will be.

How to Ask

Key, of course, is how to gather this data. Should you talk with people directly, by phone, or contact them by mail? Ideally, you would like to have face-to-face conversations with customers. What someone says is important. How they say it also is valuable. Body language, mannerisms, and tone of voice enhance your understanding of the customer's priorities.

Critical Linkages and Critical Impacts Analysis

The **Critical Linkages Analysis** and the **Critical Impacts Analysis** must be done face-to-face. People to conduct the face-to-face discussions are available from several sources. Students from a local college or university often do this type of work. You can use research professionals, your employees, and yourself. Just be sure each researcher understands how to use the survey tools, how to listen and probe, and how to collect the data.

There is one caveat. If you use your employees to collect customer data, be sure they actually get it from customers. Provide an environment that considers the amount of time required of your employees to get this information. You want to be mindful that employees already have other activities that fill their time.

Purchase Characteristics Questionnaire

A data collection option for the **Purchase Characteristics Questionnaire** is the telephone survey. In telephone surveys, be sure to identify yourself and what you are doing. Make the call non-threatening. Most people will give you some of their time. Again, you can use other people to conduct the telephone surveys. Be sure the surveyors know what they are to do and how they are to do it. Consider using professional telemarketing research organizations if you use the phone. Many times these organizations already have a data base containing your target market segments. If you use their data base, be sure you receive a copy of the list of contacts made by the telemarketers.

When possible, follow up with the customer if something is not clear or necessary data is missing. You will build your marketing strategy based on the answers to the questions, so you must be certain of your data.

Another data collection option for the **Purchase Characteristics Questionnaire** is using the mail. The advantage to this format is you can offer anonymity and, because it is less expensive, you may be able to collect a greater volume of data. The drawback to this method is there is no dialogue. Further, you need to mail many more questionnaires than you will receive back—a 5–10 percent return rate indicates a good response. Also, there is no opportunity for follow-up questions. Because of this, you need to be very precise in what you ask and how you word each question.

 ## *Action Point*

Identify customers in each market segment for face-to-face conversations. You should survey a manageable number of customers that still supplies you with a good base of information.

Complete a **Critical Linkages Analysis** and a **Critical Impacts Analysis** with each customer. Consolidate your data. Record your consolidated information on **Worksheet 2.**

Complete a **Purchase Characteristics Questionnaire** with each customer. Consolidate your data. Record the consolidated information on **Worksheet 3.**

On **Worksheet 1,** record the geographic dispersion of the customers. In other words, in what area are the customers in this market segment located? ■

Qualifying Your Market Segments

Now that you have collected data to develop information, you need to qualify your market segments. The qualification process will eliminate those segments where you have little if any opportunity to win. This is your first step in focusing on the target markets where you can win.

Consider the following questions for each market segment on your worksheets.

- Can my company satisfy the linkage priorities of the customer? (Review **Worksheet 2.**)
- Can my company satisfy the impact priorities of the customer? (Review **Worksheet 2.**)
- Via my products, services, and organization, can I satisfy the customer's needs and benefits sought? (Review **Worksheet 2.**)

Satisfying the customer means that he or she perceives value in your offering. Their need(s) will be fulfilled if they conduct business with you and purchase your products and services. Ultimately, the satisfied customer is willing to part with money to obtain your product and/or service.

These are screening questions. As such, the only market segments you will answer *no* for are the ones that are clearly *no*. Any segment where you can satisfy the customer, or think you can satisfy them, rates a *yes* answer at this point.

For those of you who answered *no* for some segments, consider the following question for those segments.

- Should I adapt or change my company, products, or services, or use an alliance with someone else to help me satisfy the customer's needs?

Here you can use some imagination. Take the example of the printer who adapted existing products to pursue the start-up business segment. Start-up businesses have to attend to many details. They need help with those details. The printer recognized the need and bundled the products necessary to open a business. This mix of products helps a start-up business owner attend to many small details.

An example of one service provider using an alliance to satisfy customer needs is a home remodeling contractor. Most home remodeling projects are either kitchen or bath makeovers. In a remodeling project a dominant customer need might be one-stop shopping. To pursue that segment and satisfy that need, the contractor may want to consider alliances. Alliances with a cabinet maker, flooring company, and a counter top company would be appropriate.

Look at the market segments where you said *no* to satisfying customer needs. Evaluate your company, products, and services, and determine if alterations and/or alliances will allow you to say *yes*.

If you still answer *no*, drop the segment from future consideration. If you cannot satisfy the needs of the customer, you cannot compete and win. Do not throw away the data you collected on market segments you are now eliminating. Save that information in a "potential future target market" file. Marketplace conditions are dynamic. They change over time for reasons you probably cannot imagine right now. As the conditions change, the market segments with customers you cannot satisfy today may be customers you can satisfy in the future. You may need to reevaluate the information you have collected. However, it will give you a good starting point.

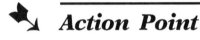 ## *Action Point*

Using **Worksheet 2A,** answer the above questions for each of your market segments. ■

Summary and Review

Selecting Target Markets is the first step in the development of a marketing and sales plan designed to increase your revenues and profits. Step One explained this process.

In this step, you had two goals:

1. to focus your efforts and resources on customers, or groups of customers, who offer the best potential for sales

2. to develop an understanding of those customers in order to better position yourself to serve those customers and provide them strong motivation to do business with you

To achieve the objectives you began with a general understanding of target marketing—the process of taking a universe of potential customers and segmenting them into manageable groups. You then explored three areas:

Segmenting Your Market

A market segment is a group of customers who share some common characteristic. The purposes behind market segmentation are to determine what groups of customers offer the best revenue and profit potential, and to help you conserve limited resources by concentrating on those customers.

You applied the following segmentation techniques to the universe of customers:

1. Vertical industries
2. Buying patterns
3. Points of purchase
4. Product mix
5. Information requirements
6. Geography

Finally, you examined common variables for segmenting consumer and commercial markets. These were:

1. Demographic characteristics
2. Psychographic characteristics
3. Operating variables

Profiling Your Customers

Next, to determine which segments offer the best revenue and profit potential, you needed to know the customers in those segments. Knowing the customers involves understanding their needs, the benefits they seek, and their purchasing characteristics.

You learned that existing businesses should begin their efforts with their present customers and then expand beyond present customers to identify segments that currently are not served.

Start-up businesses should segment based on industry knowledge, information from industry associations, and knowledge of what the competition is doing.

You compiled information on each market segment in **Worksheet 1.** To gather this information you used the following tools:

1. Critical Linkages Analysis

   A linkage is a point of connection between you and the customer. There is often more than one point of connection. Also, the importance of a linkage in the mind of the customer varies. Your goal is to identify the various linkages, and have the customer rank them in order of importance.

2. Critical Impacts Analysis

   An impact is the effect your company has on the customer in a business transaction. Your ability to perform, or not perform, can impact the customer in many ways. Your goal is to identify the impacts you have on the customer, and have the customer rank them in order of importance.

3. Purchasing Characteristics Questionnaire

   Purchasing characteristics are the requirements and attributes exhibited by your customers when they make a buying decision. Your goal is to identify those characteristics.

You need to use these three tools with a representative sampling of customers in each segment. You may query the customers face to face, via telephone, or through the mail. A face-to-face method is the best when exploring critical linkages and critical impacts.

Finally, data was compiled on **Worksheet 2** and **Worksheet 3.**

Qualifying Your Market Segments

For the sake of simplicity and manageability, you pared down the list of market segments. A series of broad questions helped you do this, and you used **Worksheet 2A.**

For each market segment you asked yourself:

- Can I satisfy the linkages?
- Can I satisfy the impacts?
- Can I meet the needs and deliver the benefits the customers seek?

If you answered *no* for any of these screening questions you asked:

- Can I adapt or form alliances that permit me to answer *yes*?

You then dropped from further consideration segments where you answered *no* to each of the above questions.

Sample worksheets and forms used in Step One are included on the following pages. Refer to each one for the proper method of completing the information.

You are now ready to move on to the second step in preparing a marketing and sales plan: Analyzing Target Markets.

Sample Worksheets

Worksheet 1

Overview for
Market Segment: *Companies w/large fleets of trucks who purchase clutches*

Description

Companies who have a fleet of trucks used for delivery, providing of services, or in

construction. Currently have 12 customers who fit this category and purchase our

clutches.

Breakdown of total customer base is:

10–25 trucks - 13 companies

26–35 trucks - 17 companies

36–50 trucks - 19 companies

51+ - 16 companies

Potential customers in segment: _____*65*_____

Total sales in segment: Last year $ ___*435,000*___

  2 yrs. ago $ ___*425,000*___

  3 yrs. ago $ ___*395,000*___

Geographic dispersion
Companies identified above are within a 50-mile radius of our location.

Date: _____

Worksheet 2

Customer Profile for Market Segment: _Fleet trucks - Clutches_

Critical Linkages

CL #1 _____ *Product quality* _____

(N,B)* _____ *High-quality products needed to keep trucks on road* _____

_____

CL #2 _____ *Inventory/availability* _____

(N,B) _____ *Must have product available when needed. Minimum turnaround time*

critical. _____

CL #3 _____ *Delivery* _____

(N,B) _____ *Need product on my site as quickly as possible. Faster I have, faster*

truck is rolling. _____

CL #4 _____ *Warranty - Need assurance of quality & recourse if defective.*

CL #5 _____ *Price - Replace a high volume of clutches. Need a reasonable price.*

CL #6 _____ *Technical support - Need to resolve installation problems quickly.*

Critical Impacts

CI #1 _____ *My deliveries* _____

(N,B) _____ *My shipping on time helps insure customer satisfaction* _____

_____

CI #2 _____ *Sales* _____

(N,B) _____ *When my fleet is rolling, my sales increase* _____

_____

CI #3 _____ *Payroll* _____

(N,B) _____ *When fleet is rolling, my payroll expense is not wasted* _____

_____

*N,B: Needs and/or Benefits Sought

Date: _____

Worksheet 2A

Initial Screening Questions
for Market Segment: _____ *Large fleets - Clutches* _____

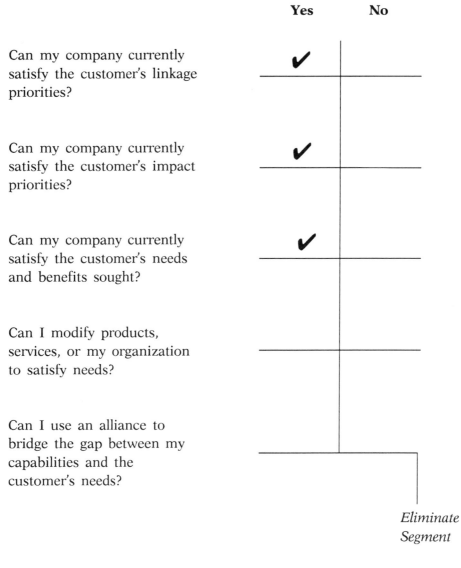

	Yes	No
Can my company currently satisfy the customer's linkage priorities?	✔	
Can my company currently satisfy the customer's impact priorities?	✔	
Can my company currently satisfy the customer's needs and benefits sought?	✔	
Can I modify products, services, or my organization to satisfy needs?		
Can I use an alliance to bridge the gap between my capabilities and the customer's needs?		

Eliminate Segment

Date: _____

Worksheet 3

Customer Profile—
Purchasing Characteristics
for Market Segment: _Large fleets - Clutches_

Point(s) of Awareness (Q1) _Referrals, trade magazines, direct mail_

Pre-sale Requirements (Q2) _Information obtained through references, salespeople, mail pieces, & advertising_

Purchase Criteria (Q3,4,5,6) _Quality of product, availability of product, delivery of product, price, warranty, reputation of supplier_

Sales Cycle (Q7) _On demand_

Price Point (Q8) _$150_

Method of Payment (Q9) _Monthly billing_

Frequency of Purchase (Q10,11) _2–3 per month_

Product Mix (Q12,13) _All parts necessary for installation_

Point of Purchase (Q14) _Dealer through delivery & over the counter_

Competition (Q15,16) _No brand recognition; major competitor - Smith Brothers_

Post-sale Requirements (Q17,18,19) _Warranty_

Date: _____

Critical Linkages Analysis

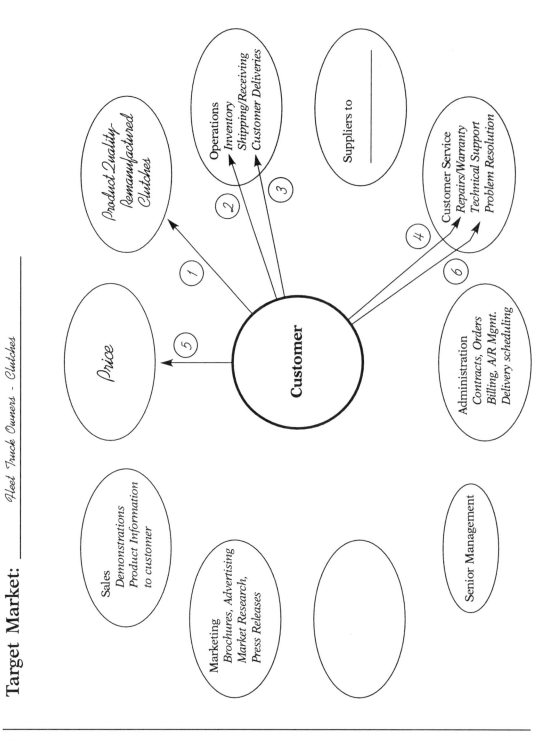

Target Market: _Fleet Truck Owners - Clutches_

- Product Quality Remanufactured Clutches
- Operations Inventory Shipping/Receiving Customer Deliveries
- Suppliers to _____
- Customer Service Repairs/Warranty Technical Support Problem Resolution
- Price
- Administration Contracts, Orders Billing, A/R Mgmt. Delivery scheduling
- Sales Demonstrations Product Information to customer
- Marketing Brochures, Advertising Market Research, Press Releases
- Senior Management

Customer

Critical Linkages Analysis

Analysis Questions

Why is linkage #1 important to your organization?

Quality of product keeps my trucks on the road.

How does this linkage benefit your business?

If trucks are down for repair, I lose sales revenue

Are there any ways you would change the nature of this linkage?

Why is linkage #2 important to your organization?

Inventory or availability of clutches minimizes my downtime on the trucks.

How does this linkage benefit your business?

Same as #1

Are there any ways you would change the nature of this linkage?

Like to have inventory on my site, and pay for it as I use it.

Critical Linkages Analysis

Analysis Questions (cont.)

Why is linkage #3 important to your organization?

Delivery is critical. When truck goes down, I need the clutch immediately.

How does this linkage benefit your business?

Same as #1.

Are there any ways you would change the nature of this linkage?

Again, like to have inventory on site.

Critical Impacts Analysis

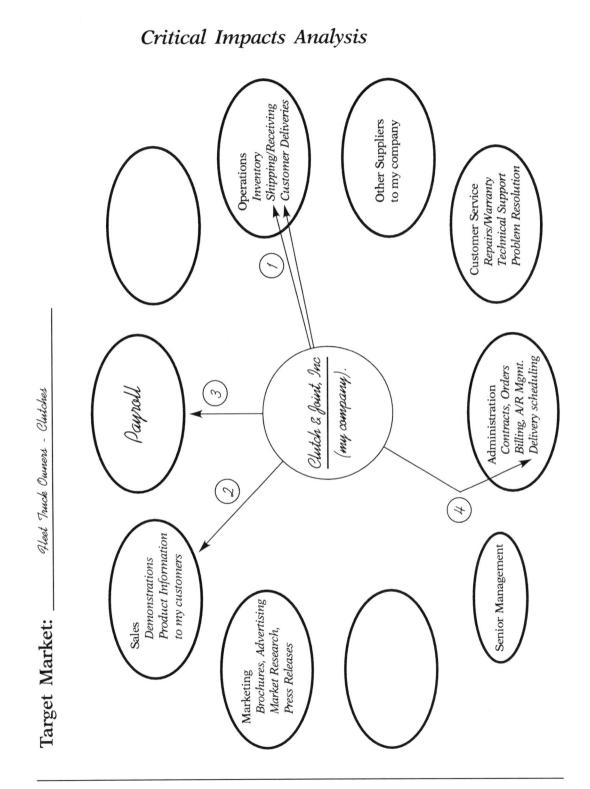

Target Market: _Fleet Truck Owners - Clutches_

Clutch & Joint, Inc _(my company)._

Operations
_Inventory
Shipping/Receiving
Customer Deliveries_

Other Suppliers
to my company

Customer Service
_Repairs/Warranty
Technical Support
Problem Resolution_

Administration
_Contracts, Orders
Billing, A/R Mgmt.
Delivery scheduling_

Senior Management

Marketing
_Brochures, Advertising
Market Research,
Press Releases_

Sales
_Demonstrations
Product Information
to my customers_

Payroll

1
2
3
4

Critical Impacts Analysis

Analysis Questions

How does the #1 impact area affect your company?

Shipping and customer deliveries are essential to my operation, my customer's satisfaction, and my cash flow.

Why is this so?

If I cannot ship product, my customers go to my competition.

If you could alter the impact, what changes would you make?

Minimize and/or specifically define the downtime for a truck needing a new clutch.

How does the #2 impact area affect your company?

Downtime on trucks decreases sales.

Why is this so?

Cannot deliver product.

If you could alter the impact, what changes would you make?

Same as #1.

Critical Impacts Analysis

Analysis Questions

How does the #3 impact area affect your company?

I have nonproductive employees when truck is down.

Why is this so?

Driver cannot deliver. I still pay him, but get no production.

If you could alter the impact, what changes would you make?

Again, minimize or finitely define downtime.

#4 Scheduling

Downtime impacts scheduling. If downtime could be controlled, scheduling could be more easily facilitated.

Purchase Characteristics Questionnaire for Products

We need your assistance. We are working to improve our products and services to you. We want to ask you some questions about *Clutches* products.

It will take about 5 minutes of your time. Will you help us?

Thank you very, very much!

Please answer the following questions while thinking about the last time you bought _*Clutches*_ .

1. Where did you first hear about or see this product?
   - Advertising
   - • Mailer
   - • Referral (friend)
   - Radio
   - Newspaper
   - Catalog
   - TV
   - Telephone sales
   - Other (Specify): _____
   - • Magazine

2. When thinking about selecting this product, where do you get information to help you make this selection?
   - Advertising
   - • Mailer
   - • From Salesperson
   - Radio
   - Other
   - • Friend
   - TV
   - Telephone sales
   - Other (specify): _____
   - • Magazine
   - Catalog
   - Newspaper
   - In Store

3. When buying this product, what feature(s) do you look for? _____
   Quality, warranty, availability, delivery

4. When comparing similar products, what do you compare? _____
   Manufacturing process, quality, warranty, availability, delivery

5. Are there any services that could help you make your purchase decision for this product?

- Information on (specify): *Supplier*
- Product demonstration
- Explain how it works
- ✔ Explain how I can install it

- Explain how I can use it
- ✔ Help me compare similar products
- Help me understand which product best suits my needs
- ✔ Referrals from other customers

6. Can you list at least five (5) criteria you use to decide to buy this product?

1	1.	*Quality*
2	2.	*Availability*
3	3.	*Delivery*
4	4.	*Price*
	5.	

Please rank these criteria in order of importance. (Use the short line next to each criteria above to indicate ranking from 1 to 5.)

7. How long a time is it from when you get interested in buying this product until you actually buy it? *Immediately*

8. When buying this product, what price range is right for you?
   From *$125* to *$150*

9. How do you usually pay for this product?

- Cash
- ✔ Expect monthly billing
- Bank loan

- Visa
- MasterCard
- Discover

- American Express
- Store card
- Other

10. How many times do you buy this product?

_____ per week or ___*2–3*___ per month or _____ per year

11. How many more times will you buy this product?

_____ Next week or ___*2–3*___ next month or _____ next year

12. What other products do you buy with this one?

None, except necessary parts to complete installation

_____

13. What other products would you like to buy with this one?

None

_____

14. Where do you usually buy this product? (Check all that apply.)
- Catalog
- Food Store
- Drug Store
- Specialty Store
- Department Store
- Discount Store
✔ • Dealer
- Other Store (specify): _____

15. When you think of this product, what brand comes to mind first?

_____

_____

16. When you think of buying this product, from where and whom do you first think to buy it?

Smith Brothers

_____

17. What result or benefits do you expect from purchasing this product?

    A truck that works
    _____

    _____

18. What services would you like after you buy this product?

    - Installation
    ✔ • Warranty
    - Instruction on: _____

    • Technical information on: _____

    _____

    Other:_____

    _____

19. How much do you think would be reasonable to pay for these services?

    Included in price
    _____

    _____

20. What is your zip code? _____

Analyzing Target Markets

In Step One you pared down the universe of market segments to target markets that offer potential. Now it is time to analyze those target markets in more depth. You need information to select the best target markets to pursue. If you do not have this information, you will be competing at a disadvantage.

You will concentrate your analysis of the target markets in two areas:

1. Your company's abilities in the target market
2. Your competitor's abilities in the target market

To complete each analysis, we will step through a series of worksheets. These worksheets are designed to work together for a clear analysis of you and your competitors' capabilities to satisfy the customer's needs in a target market.

Think of the worksheets in three groups. Group one is the customer—**Worksheets 1, 2,** and **3.** Group two is you—**Worksheets 4** and **5** with supporting information on **Worksheets A, B,** and **C.** Group three is the competition—**Worksheets 6** and **7,** with supporting information on **Worksheet D.**

Worksheets 2, 4, and **6** and **3, 5,** and **7** are summary sheets you will use for comparisons. These sheets will enable you to look quickly at a target market and see how you and the competition stack up against the linkages, impacts, needs and benefits, and purchase characteristics of the customer. Using the worksheets, you can determine if you can satisfy your customers and if you can do it better than the competition.

Your Company's Abilities in the Target Market

The profile of your company is a determination of how well you can satisfy the needs, benefits sought, and purchase characteristics of the customer in each target market.

You will first need to do **Worksheets A** and **B,** profile of your company, and **Worksheet C,** product and service analysis.

Company Profile

Worksheets **A** and **B** make up your company profile. The company profile is a picture of your business. It shows who you are and what you want to accomplish. It also defines pertinent information about your business in a simple format. This book is not intended to teach you how to do a company profile. Rather, we define the data required for the development of your marketing plan.

 Action Point

Complete your company profile. Use **Worksheets A** and **B** for this assignment. The following background information will help you successfully complete these two worksheets. ■

Goals/Objectives

Goals can be *quantitative* or *qualitative*. Quantitative goals are specific and measurable. Listed below are some typical quantitative goals. Add to the list as necessary to describe your company. Just be sure that the additions are specific and measurable.

Sample quantitative goals:

- Desired sales volume in 12 months/24 months/36 months
- Desired earnings growth rate percent per year
- Desired contribution/gross margin percent
- Desired profit after taxes percent

Qualitative goals reflect your desires for your business. They show a philosophy or strategy that is driving your efforts. Writing these goals down is important. By putting them in words, you are crystallizing your desires. This clarity of thought will be valuable as you face strategic decisions necessary to expand your business.

It will provide you with a framework upon which to structure and consider day-to-day decisions.

Same qualitative goals:

- To provide quality products backed by quality service
- To be aware of our customer's needs, and to direct our resources so we may satisfy those needs
- To treat our employees as our most important asset, and to provide an environment conducive to growth and development
- To be a responsible member of our community

Business Characteristics

Products description (1–2 sentences): A generic description of what you provide your customers, for example, a full line of replacement parts for foreign and domestic cars; high-quality, high-end audio and video components and systems; plumbing, heating, and air conditioning parts for repair and new installation.

Services description (1–2 sentences): A generic description of services you provide your customers, for example, delivery service; full warranty protection; return policy—no questions asked; planning and design help; initial consultations at no charge.

Customer segments served (1–2 sentences for each segment): A generic description of the target markets you now serve, for example, residential customers; commercial accounts; government accounts.

Location(s): A list of all company locations; stores, warehouses, distribution centers, offices, all locations where your company is resident.

Geographic area served: A description of the area your business covers.

Sales channels: A list of how you get your products and services to the customer, for example, direct sales, distributors, reps, agents, dealers, mail order, telesales.

Resources available for marketing: Take a moment to review your personnel and financial resources. You need to know what you can dedicate to your marketing efforts. List all personnel involved in marketing, and the amount of time on a daily or weekly basis they can dedicate to it. Be sure to account for yourself.

Company strengths: What are your areas of expertise?

Company weaknesses: In what areas do you lack expertise?

Analysis of Products and Services

Effectively competing means knowing your competitive tools—your products and services. Knowing your products and services involves knowing the features and benefits available from them. Knowing features is a training issue; knowing benefits is a marketing issue. Here we focus on benefits only.

First, we discuss the difference between a feature and a benefit. A feature is any attribute of a product or service. For example, engine size on an automobile, processing speed of a computer, or the range of options on a stereo system are all features. They describe some aspect of the product or service.

Benefits describe how a product or service will help a customer. Benefits may satisfy a need, meet a goal, or solve a problem. Examples include saving time, increasing efficiency, reducing payroll expense, reducing operating expenses, and increasing revenues. All of these show some net result that the customer could not realize if they did not make use of your product or service.

You can use features and benefits to differentiate your firm, your products, and your services from the competition. Later, we will explore in detail how differentiation can be an effective strategy for creating a competitive advantage. For now, suffice it to say that differentiating your product or service through the use of benefits is much more powerful than using features. Benefits help customers relate more easily to why your product is right for them. They can realize quickly what gains can be received. Benefits show customers what needs are being satisfied.

Action Point

Your analysis begins with some lists. On the top of **Worksheet C,** list the products you offer. The bottom list is for the services you offer.

For each products list the benefits the customer receives.

For each service list the benefits the customer receives. ■

Company Capabilities

You can now evaluate how well your company is equipped to satisfy the needs of your market segment(s).

Action Point

Using the information on completed **Worksheets A, B,** and **C** as a foundation, complete **Worksheets 4** and **5** for each selected target market. Indicate how well you feel you can satisfy the linkages, impacts, needs and benefits, and purchase characteristics of the customer. Indicate where you feel you have an opportunity to differentiate.

You will calculate the market share information requested on **Worksheet 4** later in this program. ■

The "opportunity to differentiate" column is where you should indicate your ability to differentiate yourself from the competition. This is the ability to distinguish yourself from the competition in the customer's mind. Differentiation is not necessarily superiority, it is uniqueness in the mind of the buyer. This uniqueness might be associated with your product capabilities, the services you offer, or how the customer buys your product. Whatever it is, it must be a difference recognized and acknowledged by the customer. Because of that difference, the customer will buy from you before he/she buys from the competition.

For now, you need to make a judgment call on your potential ability to differentiate yourself. Further along in the program, you will analyze specific differentiation capabilities and develop strategies around them.

Your Competitor's Abilities in the Target Market

A competitor is any business that offers the same or similar products and services to the same groups of customers you are targeting. You need to analyze these companies. Once you know more about them, you can develop strategies to combat them. These strategies will allow you to increase your market share and profits.

◆ Action Point

Analyze the competition by completing the profile **Worksheet D** for each competitor. ■

To gather information on the competitors, use some of the intelligence gathering techniques discussed earlier. Visit competitors' locations. Observe and talk to their customers. Become a customer of the competitor. Talk to their salespeople. Talk to their customers. Use the reference sources identified in the Appendix of this book. There are many sources available.

You need information in the following areas:

1. Location(s):
   • Where is the competition located?

- What type of facilities do they have?

2. Products offered:
   - What are the competitors' product lines?
   - What product mixes do they offer?

3. Services offered:
   - What pre-sale services are available?
   - What post-sale services are available?

4. Markets served:
   - What geography do the competitors serve?
   - What market segments do they serve?

5. Points of sale:
   - Where does the competitor sell?
   - What sales channels does the competitor use?

6. Strengths:
   - What is the competitor's area(s) of expertise?

7. Weaknesses;
   - Where does the competitor lack expertise?

➤ *Action Point*

Using the data from **Worksheet D** as a foundation, for each selected market segment complete the information on **Worksheets 6** and **7.** Show how well each competitor can satisfy the critical linkages, critical impacts, needs and benefits sought, and purchase characteristics of the customer.

Show where you believe a competitor uses a certain capability as a point of differentiation in the mind of the customer. Complete **Worksheets 6** and **7** for each competitor in each selected market segment.

You will calculate the market share information requested on **Worksheet 6** later in this program. ∎

Market Share Analysis

We define *market share* as that part of the business you received versus your competitors over a set period. For example, customers in your target market spent $2.5 million last year. Your sales to that market segment were $.5 million. That means you had a 20 percent market share for last year. So you need to know what customers spent for your type of product, by target market. You also need to know what customers spent on your competition's product, by target market.

Precise numbers are not as important as a solid idea of the market share percentages. You need to know your relative position in each target market.

How to Calculate Market Share:

There are two questions to answer. The first question is:

- What are the total sales in a target market for the product or service you sell to that market? (Determine these sales figures by year for the last three years.)

The best source for getting this information is your industry association. Tracking of sales and growth rate for an industry is standard operating procedure for its association. If an association does not exist, consult the additional reference sources noted in the appendix of this book.

While doing the research for a total sales figure, determine the number of potential customers in the target market. This information also should be readily available from the industry association. Both the total sales figures and the number of customers will be important when you rate your target markets and make your final decision on which ones to pursue.

The second question to answer is:

- What were your total sales for the corresponding years you entered for sales above?

You must determine how your business is doing in relation to the industry. This is market share. Obviously this only applies to existing businesses. If you are a start-up business, your market share is zero.

➤ *Action Point*

Answer the above two questions for each target market you are analyzing. Determine what your total sales are as a percentage of the market sales for like products or services. You have just calculated your market share. Do this on a year by year basis for comparison purposes.

As best as you can, determine the market share of your competitors. Precision is not necessary. You are attempting to determine your share of the market relative to the competitors.

Record your market share percentage in the most recent year for each target market on **Worksheet 4.**

Record your competitor's market share percentage for each target market on **Worksheet 6.**

Record the total sales for the target market on **Worksheet 1.** Record the number of potential customers for the target market on **Worksheet 1.** ■

Summary and Review

In Step Two you determined how well you and the competition stack up in your target markets. The barometer for measuring your effectiveness is the customer.

Step Two asked one important question:

- How well do you and your competitors satisfy the needs of the customers?

Your analysis started with profiles of yourself and profiles of the competitors.

Profiling Your Company

Your company profile included descriptions of the following:

- Goals
- Products
- Services
- Current customer segments
- Location
- Geographic area served
- Sales channels
- Analysis of resources

You used **Worksheets A, B,** and **C** to gather this information. You next completed **Worksheets 4** and **5.** These helped you easily compare your capabilities against the customer requirements listed on **Worksheets 2** and **3.**

Profiling Your Competitors

Your competitor's profile included descriptions of the following:

- Location(s)
- Products offered
- Services offered
- Markets served
- Points of sale
- Strengths
- Weaknesses

You compiled this information using any or all of the intelligence gathering techniques cited in the text and used **Worksheet D** to record the data.

You next completed **Worksheets 6** and **7.** Like **Worksheets 2-5,** these sheets helped you compare competitors' capabilities against yours in satisfying customer requirements.

Finally, you calculated market share for yourself and each of your competitors.

Sample worksheets and forms used in Step Two are included on the following pages. Refer to each one for the proper method of completing the information.

The next phase of your marketing and sales planning is discussed in Step Three: Rating Target Markets.

Sample Worksheets
Worksheet A

Company Profile

Goals/Objectives

Qualitative

To expand presence in fleet market

To be recognized as best customer service company in town

To create 2 new job opportunities per year

To create increased income opportunities for employees

Quantitative

Triple share of clutch business in fleet market in one year

Increase sales from $1.9 million to $2.2 million in 12 months

Double brake business in fleet market in 2 years.

Expand to a 2nd location in 4 years.

Business Characteristics

Products Description

Drive lines, brakes, and clutches for truck after market.

Numerous ancillary products.

Services Description

Warranties, delivery, technical support line

Customer Segments Served

Individual owner/operators

Small fleets - less than 10 trucks

Large fleets - greater than 10 trucks

Worksheet B

Business Characteristics (cont.)

Location(s)
One - 123 Adams St., Anytown, U.S.A.

Geographic Area Served
50 mile radius of location

Sales Channels
Over the counter sales

One salesperson for larger accounts

Resources Available for Marketing

Name	Time Hours	%
Salesperson	50	100
General manager	10	20
President	20	40
Delivery person	10	25

Company strengths/areas of expertise
Quality products, warranty, expertise of personnel, referral base,

computer system for inventory control

Company weaknesses/lack of expertise
Small size compared to competition, tight cash flow, available capital

to invest

Worksheet C

Analysis of Products and Services

Product Analysis

Description
Drive lines
Brakes
Clutches

Benefit
All products give the customer
reasonably priced, high-quality
replacement parts that extend the useful
life of their vehicle assets.

Services Analysis

Description
Warranty
Delivery
Technical Assistance

Benefit
Level of assurance and method of
recourse in the event of a defective part.
Minimized downtime on vehicles because
of prompt receipt of needed parts.
Minimal vehicle downtime because
installation problems are quickly
resolved.

Worksheet D

Business Analysis
for Competitor: _Smith Brothers_

Location(s): 2 - 1919 Jefferson St. (south half of town)

2251 McKinley Ave. (north half of town)

Products offered: Drive lines, clutches and brakes for truck after market

Services offered: Warranty, delivery, technical support, roadside assistance

Markets served: Large fleet owners

Small fleet owners

Individual owner/operators

Points of sale: Direct sales - 3 people

(Channels) Over the counter

2 retail re-sellers - 1 north & 1 south

Strengths: Longer presence in market - greater name recognition, stronger

financial position

Weaknesses: Delivery response time - high volume negatively impacts it.

Worksheet 4

Company Capabilities
for Market Segment: *Large fleets - clutches*

My Company's Market Share _____ *18* _____ %   *(12 of 65 customers)*

Ability to satisfy critical linkages   *Opportunity to differentiate?*

CL #1 ___ *Product quality - can satisfy* ___
(N,B) ___ *Established base & referrals will help in selling quality of* ___
___ *product* ___

CL #2 ___ *Inventory - can satisfy* ___   ✔
(N,B) ___ *Inventory available. Computer inventory control will help sell* ___
___ *point we will have product when needed* ___

CL #3 ___ *Delivery - semi satisfy* ___   ✔
(N,B) ___ *Limited personnel affects our delivery time. Changing point of* ___
___ *purchase to customer site inventory will help overcome this.* ___

CL #4 ___ *Warranty - can satisfy* ___
CL #5 ___ *Price - can satisfy* ___
CL #6 ___ *Technical support - can satisfy, our personnel are more* ___   ✔
___ *experienced.* ___

Ability to satisfy critical impacts

CI #1 ___ *Delivery schedule - satisfy* ___   ✔
(N,B) ___ *Customer site inventory will facilitate minimum downtime &* ___
___ *scheduling* ___

CI #2 ___ *Sales - satisfy* ___   ✔
(N,B) ___ *Customer site inventory will put trucks on the road faster. Result* ___
___ *- increased sales* ___

CI #3 ___ *Payroll - satisfy* ___   ✔
(N,B) ___ *Customer site inventory will get drivers on the road faster.* ___
___ *Result - productive payroll expense* ___

N,B: Needs and/or Benefits Sought

Date: _____

Worksheet 5

My Company's Capabilities to Meet the Purchasing Characteristics for Market Segment: _Large fleets - clutches_

Point(s) of Awareness (Q1) _Satisfy & use all media_

Pre-sale Requirements (Q2) _Satisfy & use all information sources_

Purchase Criteria (Q3,4,5,6) _Satisfy criteria. Will improve & differentiate on delivery of product through customer site inventory system._

Sales Cycle (Q7) _Satisfy_

Price Point (Q8) _Satisfy_

Method of Payment (Q9) _Satisfy_

Frequency of Purchase (Q10,11) _Can meet demand_

Product Mix (Q12,13) _Can meet requirements_

Point of Purchase (Q14) _Shifting to customer site rather than delivery or O.T.C._

Competition (Q15,16) _Smith Brothers offers no customer site inventory_

Post-sale Requirements (Q17,18,19) _Satisfy_

Date: _____

Worksheet 6

Competitor Capabilities
for Market Segment: _Large fleets - clutches_

Competitor: _Smith Brothers_   Market Share _82_ %

Ability to satisfy critical linkages   *Points of differentiation?*

CL #1 _Product quality_
(N,B) _Satisfies customer's quality requirements_

CL #2 _Inventory/availability_   ✔
(N,B) _Has a larger & broader selection of inventory_

CL #3 _Delivery_   ✔
(N,B) _Has 2 more delivery people and one more location_

CL #4 _Warranty - satisfies_
CL #5 _Price - satisfies_
CL #6 _Technical support - Personnel on average have less expertise_

Ability to satisfy critical impacts

CI #1 _Deliveries_   ✔
(N,B) _At present, faster response time_

CI #2 _Sales_   ✔
(N,B) _Faster response facilitates faster repairs for customer._

CI #3 _Payroll_   ✔
(N,B) _Faster response facilitates productive payroll expense_

N,B: Needs and/or Benefits Sought

Date: _____

Worksheet 7

Competitor ___Smith Brothers___

Capabilities to Meet Purchasing
Characteristics for Market Segment: ___Large fleets - clutches___

Point(s) of Awareness (Q1) ___Use all media___

Pre-sale Requirements (Q2) ___Use all information sources___

Purchase Criteria (Q3,4,5,6) ___Currently better on delivery.___

Sales Cycle (Q7) ___Satisfy___

Price Point (Q8) ___Satisfy___

Method of Payment (Q9) ___Satisfy___

Frequency of Purchase (Q10,11) ___Can meet demand___

Product Mix (Q12,13) ___Can meet requirements___

Point of Purchase (Q14) ___Do not offer customer site inventory___

Competition (Q15,16) _____

Post-sale Requirements (Q17,18,19) ___Satisfy___

Date: _____

Step Three

Rating Target Markets

Read this information . . .	. . . complete this Action Point
Question #1	Worksheet 8
Question #2	Worksheet 8
Question #3	Worksheet 8
Question #4	Worksheet 8
Question #5	Worksheet 8
Overall Rating of the Target Markets	Worksheet 9

You now have all of the necessary data to understand your customers in each target market. You know your products and services, your competition, and your industry position. it is now time to make the information work for you.

Via a series of questions in this step you will gauge:

1. Your resource capabilities against the demands of each target market
2. Your ability to differentiate yourself from the competition in each target market

Your answer to the following questions will tell you what competitive advantages you have. Once you answer the questions, you will rate your overall strength in each target market. You will analyze what you can expect to get from each market. Finally, you will balance all of these factors to determine which target markets offer you the best potential for revenues and profits.

You will use **Worksheet 8** to record your answers to the questions. Use one worksheet per target market.

Question #1

Do you have the resources necessary to pursue this target market successfully?

To answer this, refer to the following pieces of information:

- Critical Linkages Comparisons—**Worksheets 2** and **4,** top 3 lines
- Critical Impacts Comparisons—**Worksheets 2** and **4,** top 3 lines
- Purchase Characteristics Comparisons—**Worksheets 3** and **5**

Look at the linkages and impacts. For the critical ones, determine the resources necessary to satisfy the customer's needs. Look at the purchase characteristics. Determine the resources necessary to satisfy them.

The following examples will help you in your thought process:

- The customer expects a 1-800 service line for questions and problems. Do you have the personnel to staff it? Can you afford the monthly expense of the line?

- The customer expects delivery within 24 hours. Do you have the financial strength to afford the inventory to accomplish this? Do you have the means to make the deliveries in the customer's time frames?

- The customer expects knowledgeable assistance while making a buying decision. Do you have personnel trained specifically on what the customer needs to know?

- The customer expects 30–45 day terms for each purchase. Do you have the cash flow to support 1½–2 months of accounts receivable?

- The customer expects to buy your product and service in multiple outlets. Do you have the personnel to cover each point of sale? Do you have the inventory to cover each point of sale? Can you offer a consistent level of sales and service in each location?

If you can satisfy your customers' expectations, answer *yes* to Question #1.

If you answer *no,* consider an alliance that will permit you to answer *yes.* If an alliance is not possible, you should not pursue the target market. If you pursue a target market with inadequate resources, you will have depleted your resources in a market where you cannot win.

The following questions deal with your ability to differentiate. On **Worksheet 4,** you indicated areas where you felt you have an opportunity to differentiate yourself from the competition. You now want to take those judgment calls and pin them down.

You will assess your ability to do this in four areas: products, services, points of sale, and price.

There are two forces at work in the differentiation game—the customer needs and the competition. You want to know if you are better than the competition in satisfying needs.

Question #2

Can you gain a competitive edge by differentiating yourself on the products offered?

Differentiating yourself based on product means having a competitive edge in the customer's mind based on the product's capabilities or quality. A competitive edge occurs when the customer thinks of your products first when considering a buying decision.

Product differentiation has various subsets. Some of those are:

- Quality of features
- Variety of features
- Capabilities
- Engineering
- Workmanship
- Repair history
- Value

Any or all of these subsets may differentiate your product. The point is that it encompasses multiple areas. You need to determine if any of the areas apply to your product.

Examples of companies who differentiate on the basis of product include:

- **Mercedes Benz.** Mercedes Benz differentiates based on the quality of their car. The engineering and attention to detail in a Mercedes automobile is outstanding. The quality of the product makes Mercedes Benz a leader in the target market they pursue.
- **SONY.** SONY is much like Mercedes Benz. The engineering and features in their electronic products is some of the best available. This makes them a leader in their target market.

To examine your product's ability to differentiate, lay out **Worksheets 2, 4,** and **6,** and **3, 5,** and **7** side by side. Match your products against the critical linkages, critical impacts, customer needs and benefits sought, and purchasing characteristics of the competition.

- Do competitors use product-related issues as a point of differentiation?
- Can you use product-related issues as opportunities to differentiate?
- Are your products unique in their ability to meet the needs of the customer?

If you can differentiate based on product, answer *yes*. If you cannot, answer *no*.

Question #3

Can you gain a competitive edge by differentiating yourself on the services offered?

Differentiating yourself based on services means having a competitive edge in the customer's mind based on the advantages and benefits available through your services. A competitive edge occurs when the customer thinks of you first because of what they will gain from your services.

Examples of companies who differentiate based on service include:

- **Books & Co.** This is a retail bookstore that has received national attention because of its ability to differentiate on service. *Sloan Management Review* says, "Books & Co., a Dayton, Ohio, bookstore whose sales have grown 30 percent a year since 1984, insists that each new employee sign a performance contract that spells out the employee's service responsibilities."[7] The service at Books & Co. is outstanding. The personnel will always help you find whatever you need, and you never have a problem finding the personnel.
- **Nordstrom.** Nordstrom, a clothing speciality store, stresses customer service above everything else when training its employees. You can return any piece of merchandise bought there (or sometimes bought somewhere else!), at any time, with no questions asked. The customer is always number one at Nordstrom.

To evaluate whether you can differentiate based on services offered, lay out **Worksheets 2, 4,** and **6,** and **3, 5,** and **7** side by side. Match your services against the critical linkages, critical impacts, customer needs and benefits sought, and purchasing characteristics of the competition.

- Do competitors use service-related issues as a point of differentiation?
- Can you use service-related issues as opportunities to differentiate?
- Are your services unique in their ability to meet the needs of the customer?

If you can differentiate based on service, answer *yes*. If you cannot, answer *no*.

Question #4

Can you gain a competitive edge by differentiating yourself based on the points of sale offered to the customer?

Differentiating based on points of sale means having a competitive edge in the customer's mind because:

1. You offer the customer convenience
2. You more effectively reach the customer in comparison to the competition

Examples of companies who differentiate based on points of sale include:

- **Domino's Pizza.** Traditionally, if you wanted pizza, you had to go to the pizza parlor. Domino's differentiated itself by bringing the pizza to you. By offering convenience and effectively reaching the customer, Domino's beat the competition. This point of sale differentiation has vaulted Domino's into the top two in the pizza industry.
- **Hanes L'eggs.** Hanes took a commodity product, panty hose, and more effectively reached their customer with it.

They determined their customers, women, were repeatedly in grocery stores and drugstores. At that time, department stores were the primary point of sales for panty hose. Hanes repackaged and renamed their product L'eggs. They place L'eggs in grocery stores and drugstores. The result was a large growth in market share. A new point of sale opened up the industry. Hanes caught the competition by surprise, and L'eggs became a market leader.

To evaluate whether you can differentiate based on point of sale, lay out **Worksheets 2, 4,** and **6,** and **3, 5,** and **7** side by side. Match your points of sale against the critical linkages, critical impacts, customer needs and benefits sought, and purchasing characteristics of the competition.

- Do competitors use points-of-sale related issues as a point of differentiation?
- Can you use points-of-sale related issues as opportunities to differentiate?
- Are your points of sale unique in their ability to meet the needs of the customer?

If you can differentiate yourself via the points of sale, answer *yes.* If you cannot, answer *no.*

Question #5

Can you gain a competitive edge by differentiating yourself based on price?

Differentiating based on price means having a competitive edge in the customer's mind because of the perceived value for the price asked. According to Michael Porter, Harvard Business School, "Value is what buyers are willing to pay. Superior value stems from offering lower prices than competitors for equivalent benefits or providing unique benefits that more than offset a higher price."[8]

Examples include:

- At the upper end of the spectrum you have Rolex watches, Rolls Royce automobiles, and Joy perfume. These products provide unique benefits for which customers are willing to pay a higher price.

- At the lower end of the spectrum you have Days Inn for business travelers, Rally's fast food hamburgers, and generic brands. These products provide equivalent benefits to customers at lower price.

The key to sales success in the examples is the perceived value for the price the company is asking. Customers buy the products because they believe the benefits are worth the purchase price.

The key to long-term success is that the perception of value must be maintained. If Rolex quality were to diminish, the customer's perception of value in the product would likewise diminish. If Days Inn accommodations were to become dirty, the perception of value may be lost. A company must maintain the perception of value.

To evaluate whether you can differentiate based on price, lay out **Worksheets 2, 4,** and **6,** and **3, 5,** and **7** side by side. Match your price against the critical linkages, critical impacts, customer needs and benefits sought, and purchasing characteristics of the competition.

- Do competitors use price-related issues as a point of differentiation?
- Can you use price-related issues as opportunities to differentiate?
- Are your prices unique in their ability to meet the needs of the customer?

If you can differentiate yourself based on price, answer *yes*. If you cannot, answer *no*.

Overall Rating of Target Markets

At this point, you have completed the questions for each selected target market. Now, it is time to rate the markets and see which ones have the best potential. Use **Worksheet 9** to record your ratings.

Rating the markets is a two step procedure.

- Step One: *How good can you be in the market?*
  You are going to look at the strength of your ability to satisfy customer needs. Then you are going to rate the strength of your ability to differentiate.
- Step Two: *What can you get out of the market?*
  You are going to look at the market size and potential, and what you can hope to gain.

Step One: How Good Can You Be?

Satisfying Customer Needs

Again, compare **Worksheets 2, 4,** and **6** and **3, 5,** and **7.** Look at your ability to satisfy customer needs, your ability to establish and nurture critical linkages, your ability to have positive impacts. You need to determine if your abilities in each of these areas are strong.

Strength comes from the customers perceiving value in your products and services. They feel they will be satisfied with your offerings. They feel the price for your products and services is fair.

The more areas in which you can satisfy the customer, the stronger your position in the target market. The stronger your position, the better your chance to win. Your determining factor is the quantity in each area that you can satisfy. Implicit in the quantity is that you can satisfy the key linkages, impacts, and needs of the customer. For example, if you can satisfy eight out of ten needs, but cannot satisfy the top two, rate the market low.

 Action Point

Using the first line of **Worksheet 9,** rate the target markets according to your ability to satisfy the customer's needs, linkage requirements, and impact requirements. Your rating should be a number from 1–10 with 1 being the best. ■

Differentiating Yourself

Your purpose here is to determine what area of differentiation is the strongest. You do not want to differentiate on every factor available to you.

If you can differentiate based on products, services, points of sale, and price (*yes* to answers to questions 2–5), you have a lot of options. However, choose one primary factor upon which to differentiate yourself. This reduces confusion on the part of the customer and keeps you focused.

Your choice of differentiating factor is tied to customer needs. If a factor available to you appeals to the top customer needs, that is the factor you should choose. That is the area of differentiation that is strongest. It is strongest because you have an edge over the competition in the area that is most important to the customer. For example, a certain segment of pizza buyers want convenience. Domino's offers convenient home delivery. The home delivery (point of sale) is their primary differentiating factor.

 Action Point

For each target market, look at the differentiating factors you can consider using. Determine where a usable differentiating factor matches the needs of the customer.

For each target market where you have usable factors (product, service, point of purchase, or price), rank them from 1 to 4 on the second part of **Worksheet 9.** The item that you rank highest indicates that this offers the strongest competitive advantage as a differentiating factor.

■

Step Two: What Can You Get Out of the Market?

You need to determine what you can realize from a target market. In order to figure this out, you need to do a *sales forecast*. A sales forecast is a prediction of sales volume you expect in a specific time frame.

Many business people say it is difficult to forecast sales accurately. The reason forecasting is difficult for some people is that they do not know their customers. Your situation is different. You have put a lot of effort into getting to know your customers. That knowledge should increase your forecasting accuracy.

Forecast your sales by target market and by product or service in each target market. Sources of information to help you build your sales forecast include:

- **Historical sales.** What type of sales volume have you traditionally achieved in a specific target market?

- **Salespeople.** Poll your salespeople for forecasts of what they anticipate selling. Instruct them to forecast by customer if possible. This will aid in accuracy.

- **Customers.** Ask customers what they anticipate spending with you in the next year. Your customer's response to questions 10–12 in the **Purchasing Characteristics Questionnaire** will help here.

- **Competitors.** In your competitive research, you should have data on the business your competitors earn in the market segment. How much of that will you take from them; in what time frame?

- **Market share analysis calculations.** Included in these calculations is a figure for total sales in that target market for your products and services. That total sales figure is the market size and potential.

Once you accumulate some raw data, use the following technique to come up with your sales forecast.

 ## *Action Point*

Use the three columns on **Worksheet 9**—worst, most likely, and best case scenarios—to forecast your sales. Identify the time period for the forecast. ■

The worst-case scenario assumes everything goes wrong. You lose your most productive salesperson. Your top customer goes with a competitor. A new competitor enters the market. Your supplier goes out of business. A recession slows spending. New government regulations negatively impact your business, etc., etc. Forecast worst-case sales from this frame of mind.

The best case scenario is the exact opposite. You add a great salesperson. You get your competitor's top customer. A competitor goes bankrupt. Your suppliers keep you well stocked. The economy picks up. You get a large government contract. Forecast best-case sales from this frame of mind.

The most likely scenario is exactly what it says. Your situation will probably fall somewhere between the worst and best case. Consider your worst and best cases. Decide what is most likely to occur. Forecast your most likely sales.

Now you can begin to make some good business decisions. Balance how well you can do in a target market against what you can get out of it. There is no formula to tell you what the proper balance is. You need your judgment and the knowledge you have gained from the data you accumulated to make your decision.

 ## *Action Point*

Now you can finish the rating of your target markets on **Worksheet 9.** You will rate them A, B, or C. Base your rating on the balance between your ability to satisfy customer needs, linkages, and impacts; your ability to differentiate yourself; and the sales volume you can expect.

An A rating means the balance is very good—good marks on all factors on **Worksheet 9.** B ratings reflect less balance—one factor is weak. C ratings show poor balance—more than one factor is weak. ■

Summary and Review

Step three is where you started to make the data work for you. You:

- Determined if you have the resources necessary to serve a market effectively
- Determined how you want to position or differentiate yourself in a market
- Ranked each of the markets so you can decide which ones to pursue

You used the data about the customers, yourself, and the competition (**Worksheets 2–7**) to answer a series of questions for each market segment you were considering. The questions helped you achieve the objectives listed above.

Identifying Resource Requirements

Question #1: Do you have the resources necessary to pursue this target market successfully?

Identifying Differentiation Opportunities

Question #2: Can you gain a competitive edge by differentiating yourself on the products offered?

Question #3: Can you gain a competitive edge by differentiating yourself on the services offered?

Question #4: Can you gain a competitive edge by differentiating yourself based on the points of sale offered to the customer?

Question #5: Can you gain a competitive edge by differentiating yourself based on price?

Rating the Markets

Question #1: How good can you be in the market?

How good you can be is a factor of your ability to satisfy customer needs, combined with your ability to differentiate yourself.

If you can satisfy the customer's needs, especially the critical ones, and you have a strong case for differentiation, you should rate the market high.

Again, the information on **Worksheets 2–7** helped you answer this question.

Question #2: What can you get out of the market?

Determining what you can get involves developing a sales forecast.

For each market, you developed a sales forecast using the best, most likely, and worst case methodology.

Overall Rating of the Markets

You assigned an overall rating to each market based on two factors. The first factor is how good you can be in a market. The second factor is what you can get out of the market.

There is no formula to tell you what the best combination should be. Using your knowledge of the customers, yourself, and the competition you determined which markets provide you the best opportunity to win.

Ultimately, you assigned each market one of the following ratings:

- A—Primary market to pursue
- B—Secondary market to pursue
- C—Future market to pursue

Sample worksheets and forms used in Step Three are included on the following pages. Refer to each one for the proper method of completing the information.

You now know who your best potential customers are by target market. You can feel good because your knowledge level is greater than the majority of business owners. That gives you an edge—it helps you win. Let's conclude with Step Four: Developing Sales Plans.

Sample Worksheets
Worksheet 8

Final Screening Questions
for Market Segment: _____

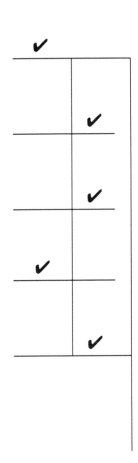

	Yes	No*
1. Do you have the resources to pursue this target market?	✔	
2. Can you gain a competitive edge by differentiating on products?		✔
3. Can you gain a competitive edge by differentiating on services?		✔
4. Can you gain a competitive edge by differentiating on points of purchase?	✔	
5. Can you gain a competitive edge by differentiating on price?		✔

*If you answer *no* to question #1, eliminate the segment; if you answer *yes* to #1, but *no* to *all* of the remaining questions, eliminate the segment.

Eliminate
Segment

Worksheet 9

Final Rating for Market Segment: _Large fleets - clutches_

How good can I be?

Ability to meet needs (1–10): _____9_____

Ability to differentiate:

Rank from 1 to 4: _____3_____ Products

_____2_____ Services

_____1_____ Points of purchase

_____3_____ Price

What can I get out of it?

				Revenues
Sales Forecasts	Best	30 customers per	year	$162,000
	Likely	25 customers per	year	135,000
	Worst	20 customers per	year	108,000

Average annual revenue per customer - $5,400

Overall rating for target market (A, B, or C): _____A_____

Step Four

Developing Sales Plans

It is now time to plan how you will go about winning customers and beating the competition in your selected market segments. You will develop a sales plan for each target market.

To do this, we will discuss the following:

- Explanation of marketing strategies
- Selection of a marketing strategy for each target market
- Explanation of the sales process
- Explanation of sales tactics
- Development of your sales plans

Marketing Strategies

The marketing strategy is an approach to a market segment. It is a direct reflection of your position in the market in relation to your competition. The marketing strategy helps prioritize your goals and the tactics to achieve those goals.

You have four choices for marketing strategy:[9]

1. Defensive
2. Offensive
3. Flanking
4. Guerrilla

Defensive Strategy

A defensive strategy can be employed by only one firm—the market segment leader. There can be only one: McDonald's in fast food restaurants, *Business Week* in business magazines.

Market share is a good indicator of the leader, but customer perception of who is the leader is the best indicator.

If you are number one in your segment, you dominate the competition. Your strategy should be defensive. Again, the determining factor is whether you are the market leader.

If you are the market leader, your goal is to maintain or increase market share. You employ two principles:[10]

1. Attack yourself

2. Counter any competitive moves

Attacking yourself requires courage. Do not become complacent with your top position. Look for your weaknesses and always strive for improvement. Based on customer needs, try to obsolete your products and services through improvement and new introductions. If you are your own critic, you will stay ahead of the competition and maintain your leadership position.

Competitive moves impinge on the leader's market. Your ability to recognize and respond to these moves will allow you to maintain a leadership position. Any competitive move that you do not challenge means you, as the leader, have relinquished that part of your market. This does not mean you must always respond. It does mean you need to make a conscious decision to respond or not. You may *choose* to relinquish part of your market to competitors.

Offensive Strategy

An offensive strategy is employed by the number two or three firm in a market segment. These are the firms recognized as strong, but not as the leader. Generally, there are only one or two in a market: Burger King and Wendy's restaurants, *Fortune* and *Forbes* magazines.

As a strong number two or three, your goal is to increase market share. Remember, when you increase your market share, in most cases you are reducing a competitor's market share.

You employ three principles in an offensive strategy:[11]

1. Focus on the leader, not yourself

2. Find a weakness in the leader's strength and exploit it

3. Attack on a narrow front—a single point only

The leader is who you attack. Keep your focus on it—its products, its pricing, its distribution, etc. To substitute your product for the leader's in the customer's mind, you must know as much as you can about the leader.

Determine a weakness in the leader's strength. That is correct—a weakness in the leader's strength. As strong as a leader's position may be, there are always weaknesses in it. Identify those weaknesses and concentrate on taking advantage of them.

The classic story that illustrates this is the attack mounted by Pepsi in the 1930s. Until that time, Coke dominated the soft drink industry. They distributed their product in the 6½ ounce bottle. The bottle became part of Coke's image. Pepsi came along and mounted an offensive strategy based on this bottle. They introduced the 12-ounce bottle. Their slogan:

> *Pepsi-Cola hits the spot.*
> *Twelve full ounces, that's a lot.*
> *Twice as much for a nickel, too.*
> *Pepsi-Cola is the drink for you.*

Part of Coke's strength was the image of its bottle. Pepsi attacked that strength. To respond to this attack, Coke had to change its manufacturing, handling, and distribution mechanics. That was expensive and time-consuming. Meanwhile, Pepsi gained market share. Today Coke and Pepsi compete head-to-head in the soft drink market. Coke has never recovered the share of the market it lost over fifty years ago.[12]

Keep your point of attack narrow. If the competitor's weakness is a capability of the product, focus on that. If the weakness involves service, for example long lines of customers, focus on that. (Remember Avis attacking Hertz' long lines for car rentals?) If the weakness is price, focus on that. Do not try to compete on all issues—choose one and concentrate on it.

Flanking Strategy

A flanking strategy is employed by the second tier in the market segment—companies that are not the leaders and not the number two or three firms in the market, yet not small players. Examples are: Rally's and Subway restaurants, *Inc.* and *Entrepreneur* magazines.

With flanking, you are trying to strengthen your position and gain market share. Successful flanking requires resources. If your resources are limited, avoid this strategy. Flanking is the most inventive form of marketing because you are usually going after a market that does not exist until you create it.

There are three principles of flanking strategy:[13]

1. Make a move into an uncontested area

2. Have surprise on your side

3. Sustain your marketing effort after the initial introduction (that's why you need resources)

Successful flanking requires creating something new. This does not necessarily mean a new product. You can flank based on distribution channel. You can flank based on product capability. The key thing to remember is that whatever factor you choose, it must be new.

Do not telegraph your flanking strategy. Surprise is critical because the competition will react. You do not want them to react before you can introduce your strategy. If they do react, you no longer have a flank; the competitor does. Only one surprise attack or flank is available at a time. Therefore, flanking is high risk— and potentially high reward. You must move fast.

Once you begin pursuing a flanking strategy, do not let up. You want to capture as much as you can as rapidly as you can. This requires a sustained effort. You want to create a firm position in the customer's mind before the competition reacts. So as your flank starts to work, pour it on.

Guerrilla Strategy

A guerrilla strategy is employed by the small players in a market segment—a local hamburger restaurant on the corner, or local business publications. Guerrilla strategies take victories where they can. They change or move on when the competition reacts.

There are three principles in guerrilla strategies:[14]

1. Find a segment or niche small enough to defend

2. Do not act like a leader

3. Withdraw when the big players start to move in

A defendable segment or niche is one that larger firms would find difficult to enter or would not want to attack. You can define the niche by geography, sales volume, specific customer group, customer size, product line specialization, or even price. What you are trying to do is severely limit the market size so you can set up a strong position.

Small, lean, and mean has tactical advantages. Keep those attributes. They give you the quickness needed to respond to changing conditions in the marketplace. That ability to respond quickly gives you a tactical advantage.

If your niche attracts competitive attention and the competitors have resources that can overcome you, it is time to move on. The worst position for a guerrilla to be in is defending a position that drains all of its resources. For guerrillas, a niche market basically is indefensible because of lack of resources.

Selecting a Marketing Strategy for Each Target Market

Action Point

Based on your position in each target market, determine your marketing strategy for each.

To determine your position, review **Worksheets 4** and **6**—market share percentage.

In each target market for which you are developing a sales plan, determine your market share in relation to the competition. Identify who the number one player in the market is. Identify numbers two and three. Identify who the other players are. Identify where you are. Based on your position in relation to the competition, select the appropriate marketing strategy. Record your selection on **Worksheet 10.** ∎

Now, you can develop specific tactics to carry out your marketing strategy. This is where you are going to convert all of your analyses and strategic decisions into action plans.

There are two principles you need to remember when developing tactics:

1. The customers are an integral part of marketing and sales planning because they provide you feedback. You must remain in constant contact with them, and they must have a method to remain in contact with you. If this does not occur, you have no idea how you are doing. You also have no way of knowing how you should adapt as the needs of the customers change.[15]

2. The purpose of a marketing and sales plan is to get customers.

Explanation of the Sales Process

Getting customers is a process. The process involves taking suspects (your target markets) and converting them into prospects (qualified leads). You then try to turn the prospects into customers (assets of the company). You try to convert the customers into repeat customers (strong assets of the company). This movement of suspects to prospects to customers to repeat customers requires a sales process.

Integrate these two criteria into your tactical planning: the feedback loop for customers, and the sales process. This means that every step of the sales process needs some type of feedback mechanism built into it.

A typical sales process can be broken down into some simple steps. They are:[16]

- Awareness
- Comprehension
- Conviction
- Order
- Reorder

Awareness

The target market is unaware of your product or service, or you. Your task is to build awareness, perhaps name recognition.

Comprehension

The target market may be aware of you, but they do not know much more. Your task is to educate the potential customers as to your products and services. You need to let them know what you can do.

Conviction

The target market understands your products and services but they have no conviction to buy. Your task is to instill conviction in the potential customers and make them believe that purchasing from you is the right thing to do.

Order

The target market believes in your products and services but may not have bought them. Your task is to get the order.

Reorder

The target market has ordered from you. You want to keep them as customers. Your task is to get them to reorder.

Explanation of Sales Tactics

How are you going to move potential customers through the sales process? How are you going to maintain a dialogue with them (remember, dialogue is two-way communication)? Through *sales tactics*. Sales tactics can be broken down into five basic groups. They are publicity, advertising, personal selling, sales promotions, and feedback mechanisms.

Publicity

Publicity is timulating demand for a product or service by planting significant news about it in a published medium or getting favorable presentation of it on radio or TV. Examples include:

- News releases
- Articles in magazines, journals, etc.
- Product reviews
- Open houses
- Speaking engagements
- Interview shows
- Sponsorship of community events
- Seminars
- Workshops
- Service club memberships
- Other club memberships

Advertising

Advertising is any paid form of non-personal presentation of a product or service. Examples include:

- Radio
- Television
- Print
  Newspapers
  Magazines
  Shoppers
  Yellow Pages

Special directories:
    Chamber of Commerce
    Trade or industry directors

- Outdoor billboards
- Cooperative ads with vendors
- Direct mail
- Direct response
- Catalogs
- Bill stuffers
- Newsletters sales or product announcements
- Brochures

Personal Selling

Personal selling is personal presentation of a product or service in a conversation with one or more prospective buyers. Examples include:

- Direct sales force
- Manufacturers' reps (agents)
- Dealers
- Storefronts
- Distributors
- Telemarketing
- Customer service sales
- Trade shows
- Mix of the above

Sales Promotions

Sales promotions are short-term incentives to encourage the purchase of a product or service. Examples include:

- Special offers
- Coupons

- Special financing
- Contests
- Rebates

Feedback Mechanisms

Feedback mechanisms are methods available to customers to provide you information about your performance, products, services, and their needs. Examples include:

- Direct questions
- Direct response advertising
- Direct mail/direct response
- Focus groups
- User groups
- Appreciation meetings
- Questionnaires
- Customer audits—mail or phone
- Lost order analysis and review
- Salespeople
- Service personnel
- Administrative personnel

Developing Your Sales Plan

How do you determine which tactics to use? By developing a sales plan. The following graphic depicts the components of a sales plan and how they interact with each other. Customer position in the sales process (suspects, prospects, etc.) dictates the response you need to elicit (awareness, comprehension, etc.). You elicit the desired response and move customers through the sales process with sales tactics. During this entire process, feedback mechanisms you have put in place are allowing you and the customer to stay in contact. You know how you are doing and where the customer is because he or she is telling you.

Sales Promotion Plan

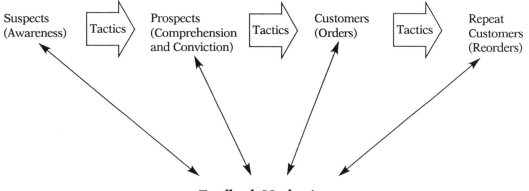

Developing your sales plan involves seven steps:[17]

1. Identify your target markets
2. Define your goals in relation to your target market strategy
3. Define the message
4. Select tactics
5. Set up a budget
6. Develop an implementation schedule for each target market
7. Measure your results

You have already identified your target markets, so we will discuss the last six of these in detail here.

Define Your Goals in Relation to Your Target Market Strategy

Your goal for each one of your target markets is to own that market. Two factors impact attaining your goal:

1. The marketing strategy for the target market
2. The customer's current location in the sales process

The following is a discussion of the relationship between marketing strategy and customer location in the sales process.

Employing a Defensive Strategy

First priority is to get orders and reorders for existing products and services. Employing a defensive strategy means that you are an existing business that can focus on your current customers. Employ tactics that will elicit orders and reorders.

Second priority is to get new customers for existing products and services. Expand your presence in target markets where there is a need for your products and services. Since these are new customers, you will have to employ tactics that create awareness. Following that, you move the prospects through the other steps of the sales process.

Third priority is a result of your examining and attacking yourself. You are creating product and service innovations. The innovations may appeal to both existing and new customers. You need to create awareness about the innovations. You need to create awareness about the innovations. Following awareness, you move your prospects through the other steps of the sales process.

The tactical key to a defensive strategy is to maintain and strengthen your position with existing customers and win new customers through innovation.

Employing an Offensive Strategy

Here, you are attacking the weakness in the leader's strength. That means you are trying to get someone else's customers. This dictates that you create awareness and comprehension on the part of these new customers about your new strength. Your new strength is the counterpart to the leader's weakness.

You then get the leader's customers by employing tactics to elicit conviction and orders. During this process do not ignore your existing customers. Continue to employ tactics that create orders and reorders.

The tactical key to an offensive strategy is to launch a surgical assault on a single point of strength (weakness). You want new customers—the leader's customers. You feel you have the strength to get them. While doing this, protect yourself by strengthening your position with your existing customers.

Employing a Flanking Strategy

You are creating something new, and you are going after new customers. You must create awareness and comprehension in the minds of those customers.

Your actions will usually bring a response from the competition, so speed is of the essence. You quickly need to develop customer conviction and orders. Your key is to set up a strong position with your innovation before the competition reacts.

As your success grows, maintain your aggressiveness. Do not let up—this provides an opening for competitors. As you receive orders, solidify your position with tactics that create reorders.

While implementing your flanking strategy, you still need to pay attention to your existing customers. Continue to employ tactics with them that bring orders and reorders.

Employing a Guerrilla Strategy

The tactics you use will be dependent on how long you have been in the market segment. If you already have market presence, use tactics that create conviction, orders, and reorders.

If you are just entering the segment, you need to move prospects through the entire sales process. Your initial tactics should focus on awareness and comprehension, and then conviction, orders, and reorders.

Define the Message

The three criteria for success in a target market are:

1. Knowing the customers needs
2. Having the ability to satisfy the customer's needs
3. Satisfying the customer's needs in a way that is better than the competition (differentiation)

Your message should reflect these criteria. The message should define your ability to satisfy the customer's needs and explain your differentiation. The purpose of the message is to gain a position in the customer's mind. Simplicity will serve you well here.

 ## *Action Point*

To determine what to include in your message, review **Worksheets 2, 4, 6,** and **3, 5, 7.** Look at your strengths in satisfying the customer's needs. Review **Worksheet 9.** Review the areas of strength for differentiating yourself from the competition.

Incorporate the information from the worksheets mentioned into a message that communicates to the customer the value associated with doing business with you. Record the message you will communicate on **Worksheet 10.**

Advertising agency personnel understand designing messages. Their expertise may help and serve as a good resource for this task. ■

Selecting Tactics

Sales tactics reflect your goals in relation to your market strategy. The tactics chosen must help you elicit the response(s) you desire.

Below are examples of tactics and feedback mechanisms that can be effective for each step of the sales process. These are only examples. Your situation is unique. Treat it as such. Use the examples to stimulate your thinking process.

Creating Awareness

Effective tactics:

• News releases
• Articles/interviews

- Advertising
- Direct mail announcements
- Sales promotions
- Catalogs
- Open houses
- Seminars
- Trade shows

Effective feedback mechanisms:

- Audits of the target market by phone or mail
- Questionnaires for all new customers
- Response to sales promotion
- Standard questions for all customers
- Training of administrative and service personnel to question customers
- Direct response advertising

Creating Comprehension

Effective tactics:

- Personal selling to interested prospects
- Targeted advertising with a specific message
- Workshops with the target market
- Telemarketing campaign with the target market
- Second level direct mail campaign
- Seminars
- Trade shows

Effective feedback mechanisms:

- Direct questions
- Training of administrative and service personnel to question customers
- Focus groups

- Questionnaires in a direct mail campaign
- Customer audits by mail or phone

Creating Conviction

Effective tactics:

- Personal sales
- Rebates
- Coupons
- Contests
- Trade shows

Effective feedback mechanisms:

- Direct questions by sales personnel
- Direct mail with direct response
- Questionnaires
- Focus groups
- Direct questions by administrative and service personnel

Creating Orders and Reorders

Effective tactics:

- Personal sales
- Sales campaign by service personnel
- Telemarketing campaign
- Direct mail sales promotion
- Trade shows
- Seminars
- Coupons
- Rebates
- Contests

Effective feedback mechanisms:

- Direct questions of customers by all personnel
- User groups
- Focus groups
- Appreciation meetings
- Questionnaires
- Regular service calls and customer audits
- Lost order analysis and review

✦ *Action Point*

Your sales strategy and your customer's position in the sales process will steer you to tactics to elicit desired responses. Be sure the tactic has built into it some method to create a dialogue with the customer—a feedback mechanism.

Determine the tactics and feedback mechanisms you will use to obtain the desired responses. Record this information on **Worksheet 11.** ■

Set Up a Budget

This is a difficult issue to address. Do you spend based on what you can afford? Do you spend based on a percentage of sales? Do you spend to match the competition? Setting up a budget based on the above criteria has problems associated with it.

If you start based on what you can afford, you are not viewing your sales promotion as an investment. Long-range planning is difficult.

If you spend based on a percentage of sales, you are using circular logic. You spend more when your sales increase, but you spend less when you do not have sales. This reduced spending may or may not be appropriate to your circumstances.

If you spend to match the competition, you are letting your competitor set your budget. Also, you are assuming the competition knows the target market as well as you do. You are also assuming they have thought through their promotion strategy as well as you have. That may not be the case.

The best method for setting up a promotion budget is to tie your budget to your promotion goals and your resource capabilities. Let's say you have identified five target markets to pursue. Each one of them requires 30 percent of your total resources to win in the market. You have a problem. Five times thirty percent is 150 percent; you do not have 150 percent of your resources. To solve the problem, you need to identify resource requirements for the target markets. You then need to compare your resources against the resources required:

This program is going to look at resource requirements in only two areas:

1. The costs and expenses associated with the target markets
2. Their effect on your cash flow

To examine your resource requirements, you will need to have the following information available:

- Profit and loss statement
- Balance sheet
- Cash flow statement
- Breakeven analysis

You incur the expenses and costs associated with the target markets in various areas. Among those areas are:

- Expense of sales tactics—advertising, promotions, telemarketing, etc.
- Number of points of sale to cover
- Number of customers to serve
- Inventory requirements
- Order processing requirements
- Accounts receivable to support

- Manufacturing costs, cost of goods, or sales expenses
- Personnel to support increased sales

Revenues from increased sales usually give you financial support for these areas. But, you have to spend the money first in order to sell the product. That means cash flow. Your cash flow is going out before the revenues come in. You need to have the cash reserves to support that time difference.

Let's go back to Domino's pizza as an example. Domino's decides to offer home delivery. Before they receive the first dollar of revenue from a home-delivered pizza, there are expenses they will incur. They need to pay for local advertising, increased inventory to support projected increases in sales, drivers' insurance, and possibly a vehicle, unless supplied by an employee.

Each of these are variable expenses associated with the strategy of pursuing the home delivery market segment. Domino's needs to factor these costs into their operating expenses and cash flow requirements. They need to know the cash requirements to introduce this new service.

The same applies to your business. You need to identify the expenses and costs you will incur in order to pursue your target market. You need to determine your cash requirements.

Also, you need to know the time frame between the sale of your product and receipt of payment. The cash demands that occur in that time frame must be funded.

For existing businesses, your financial statements should contain the data you need. Look at your profit and loss (P&L) statement to determine the cash demands of your target market. Review your cash flow statement to determine the time frame you need to fund. If you do not have a cash flow statement, use your accounts receivable schedule.

For start-up businesses, consider doing your pro forma financial projections to assess the demands of each target market. Your industry association, your franchisor, or your market research should help you determine the time frame you must fund.

For both existing and start-up businesses, consider using accountants. Their expertise could be invaluable in this analysis.

➤ *Action Point*

Start with the target market that offers the best potential. Determine what expenses and costs you will incur to pursue that market. Determine your cash requirements. Proceed in the same manner for each target market.

On **Worksheet 12,** record the expense information for your target market. Compare your available resources to the demands of the market. Determine what you can afford to do and assign and assign a monthly budget figure to pursue that target market. ■

Develop an Implementation Schedule for Each Target Market

You now need to lay out a schedule for putting the sales tactics into effect. The schedule indicates when you will implement each tactic.

When determining your schedule, be sure to consider your resources. Do not schedule tactics and activities that overextend your capabilities. For example, do not schedule 100 new personal selling contacts per salesperson per week. That is not reasonable. Overextending capabilities results in poor execution and poor customer service.

Be sure someone is responsible for each tactic you implement. Your expectations regarding the implementation of the tactic should be spelled out and clearly understood by all personnel involved.

Stay focused in your implementation scheduling. Do not schedule too many programs simultaneously. Going in too many directions usually results in confusion and less than satisfactory results. It may also reflect a lack of direction on your part.

Put in place systems to support your marketing efforts. Systems are procedures in your company for tracking results, handling data, and supporting and servicing the customer. For example, if you advertise, track the number of leads you get per advertising medium. Have a method in place to handle the leads you receive. Insure that you can track the lead to one of two conclusions—a customer or a lost order. If a customer results, make sure the service they receive is outstanding. Have a feedback mechanism available to the customer. If you design your marketing programs to increase business, the last thing you want is for internal problems to interfere with business.

Action Point

Develop an implementation schedule for each target market. Record the implementation schedule on **Worksheet 13.** Identify the person responsible for executing each tactic.

Compare the schedules for your target markets. Review them for conflict. If conflicts exist, change the implementation schedules. ■

Measure Your Results

Customer Satisfaction

You have gone to a lot of effort to include feedback mechanisms in your sales tactics. *Use* the feedback. Your customers will always be the best source of information as to how you are doing. Listen to them.

Train all employees on effective customer dialogue. Every contact between an employee and a customer is marketing. Every contact leaves an impression on the customer. You want that impression to be the best possible. To accomplish that, your employees need to know what they should do and how to do it.

Customer complaints are an opportunity to gain a customer's confidence. It all depends upon how you and your employees handle them. Consider special training in this area.

Develop a system to monitor your employees' interface with your customers. The system can be a simple audit. It can be observation by management. It can be written forms the employees complete. It can be written feedback from the customers. Do not use the system to discipline employees. Rather, it should help you in training employees by pointing out deficiencies in your customer service.

When seeking feedback from your customers, do not be intrusive. Your customer is a valuable asset. You do not want to jeopardize that asset through overuse. Provide your customer an easy way to give you feedback. For example, prepare one to three short questions that a customer can answer whenever they make a purchase. The questions should address the critical functions in your business that satisfy the customer's needs.

- If *speed* is a need, ask—Did we deliver on time?
- If *information* is a need, ask—Did you get all of your questions answered?
- If *quality* is a need, ask—Were you pleased with the results?

The questions can be verbal or written, depending on which is more appropriate.

Always get the name, address, and phone number of every customer. Remember, customers are assets. If you were handed $100, would you forget where you put it? Similarly, don't forget your customer.

Knowing every customer is valuable in many ways. It is much easier to get a reorder from an existing customer than it is to get a new customer. Existing customers can help you get new customers. Existing customers can be your best ongoing source of feedback.

Financial Results

To this point, I have addressed measuring results in terms of customer satisfaction. The other side to results is the financial performance of the company. You selected target markets based on your ability to increase revenues through satisfying needs and differentiating yourself from the competitors. You need to know whether those increased revenues are becoming reality.

There are several indicators to measure the financial results of your plans. First, your P&L statement will show your revenues. Track the revenues over time and see if they are increasing. (If possible, departmentalize your P&L statement by target market. Your accountant can assist you with this. If you can do this, you can analyze each target market as a stand-alone profit center.)

A second indicator is number of customers. If that is increasing, your plans are producing some positive results.

A third method for measuring your results is to track the effectiveness of a specific tactic. I discussed earlier tracking the number of leads generated by a specific advertising medium. That is one example. Another example might be your close rate. What percentage of sales calls produce orders? If it improves, your understanding of the customer and message content is probably good. If it declines, examine the customer feedback (e.g., lost order review) to see where the problem lies.

Do not conclude that a target market is not worth pursuing if you do not realize financial improvement in a short time frame. Give yourself at least six months to see if your assessment of a target market is correct. If improvement is not there, and not projected to be there, review your analysis. Look at the customer's feedback. Incorporate that feedback. Many variables affect success or failure. Try to account for as many variables as possible before abandoning a target market.

Implementation

Good marketing is important for success. Good execution of the strategies is also important. The purpose of this program is to help you develop a thoughtful, workable marketing plan. However, it would be remiss not to address the issue of the execution of that plan.

If you do not execute well, even the best strategies can fail. Thomas Bonoma, in *The Marketing Edge*, presents a diagram that shows the relationship between strategy and execution. That diagram is reproduced here.

Execution is:	Strategy is: Appropriate	Strategy is: Inappropriate
Good	Success: All that can be done to assure success has been done.	Roulette: Good execution can mitigate poor strategy, forcing management to success. *or* The same good execution can hasten failure.
Poor	Trouble: Poor execution hampers good strategy. Management may never become aware of strategic soundness because of execution inadequacies.	Failure: Very hard to diagnose, because bad strategy is masked by poor execution. Even harder to fix, because two things are wrong.

The underlying premise of Bonoma's theory is that implementation is more important than strategy when trying to diagnose problems. It is impossible to evaluate strategy when implementation is suspect.[18]

The most interesting cells in Bonoma's diagram are the secondary diagonal cells where mismatches occur. If strategy is appropriate, but execution is poor, "trouble" results. You cannot assess the adequacy of a strategy if the ability to implement it is poor.

In the opposite scenario, good execution coupled with poor strategy results in "roulette." This makes it difficult to predict consequences. If there is good implementation of a poor strategy, the failure of the program or company could take place quite quickly. On the other hand, good implementation could modify the strategy to negate the poor aspects of it. Despite a poor strategy, a good implementer could turn it into a success.[19]

Two points are critical in Bonoma's theory. First, you should distinguish implementation problems from strategic problems. This is possible and relatively easy to do. Second, it is important you do so, because you cannot assess the adequacy of a strategy without being able to implement effectively. "When in doubt, the analysis recommends, look first to implementation problems and fix them, so that strategic adequacy can be more clearly seen."[20]

Bonoma outlines three issues that affect the success or failure of marketing programs.[21]

1. Empty promises marketing—This occurs when management creates programs the organization cannot execute due to a lack of resources or a lack of personnel.

2. Bunny marketing—This occurs when management is unclear in its marketing thinking and direction. It masks this lack of clarity by implementing a multitude of programs or tactics, hoping one or more will work.

3. A profusion of failed marketing programs can usually be tied to top management who did not provide a strong theme, direction, or culture for their marketing efforts.

Make sure you can execute the tactics you plan. Equip your people so they can execute. Insure understanding throughout the organization. Keep top management involved in the creation and implementation.

Summary and Review

Step Four discussed the conversion of your knowledge into intelligence—intelligence on how to get customers. Your goals were:

- Understanding the components of a sales plan: marketing strategy, the sales process, sales tactics, the and sales plan process.
- Developing a sales plan for each target market you wanted to pursue.

Marketing Strategy

You have one of four choices for a marketing strategy:

- Defensive
- Offensive
- Flanking
- Guerrilla

Your position in a market relative to your competition dictates what marketing strategy you choose.

Sales Process

The sales process is the path for turning suspects into prospects into customers and repeat customers. Each step in the path reflects the customer's mind set with regard to you and your products and services. A customer can be in one of four positions in the process:

- Awareness
- Comprehension
- Conviction
- Orders and reorders

Sales Tactics

Sales tactics are tools you use to move customers through the sales process. These tools help you convert a customer's mind from one state to a more desirable state. They also help you know if you are accomplishing your goal. Sales tactics fall into one of five categories:

- Publicity
- Advertising
- Personal selling
- Sales promotions
- Feedback mechanisms

Sales Plan Process

The sales plan process is the combination of a marketing strategy, the sales process, and sales tactics. This combination creates customers.

The marketing strategy helps you identify where customers are in the sales process. Sales tactics help you move customers through the sales process. The successful combination of the above elements creates customers.

Developing a Sales Plan

Developing a sales plan is a seven step process. The steps are:

1. Identify target markets to pursue
   You accomplished this in the first three steps of the program.

2. Select a marketing strategy
   You thought about your market share position, your knowledge of the customers, and your ability to differentiate. Combining these elements helped you determine a marketing strategy.

3. Define your sales message
   You asked yourself: What do I want to tell the customers to position myself in their minds?

4. Select sales tactics
   Based on the strategy you wanted to employ, what was your customer's present position in the sales process? You selected tactics and feedback mechanisms to move customers through the sales process.

5. Set up a budget
   You determined what tactics and feedback mechanisms you could afford.

6. Develop an implementation plan
   You identified realistic time frames in which to put into effect your sales tactics. You also identified points of responsibility in your organization for each step in the implementation plan.

7. Measure results
   Finally, you listened to what the customers told you, tracked your results, and adjusted your plan, if necessary, based on the customer's feedback.

Sample worksheets and forms used in Step Four are included on the following pages. Refer to each one for the proper method of completing the information.

Sample Worksheets
Worksheet 10

Strategy for Market Segment: *Large fleets - clutches*

Market Strategy (choose one):

Defensive (#1): _____

Offensive (#2, #3): _____

Flanking (#3–5, with resources): ✔ _____

Guerrilla (small player): _____

Market Message:

Our innovation is a new point of purchase - the customers location. We will stock on the customer's site a minimum monthly inventory requirement for the clutches they use. As used, we will deliver replacements. Our computer system will maintain customer inventory, delivery and billing records. Customer is no longer waiting 2 hours to one day for delivery of needed parts. They just pull them off their shelf. We contact customer minimum twice per week for replacement requirements. We issue a monthly bill for inventory used. Payment terms - 10 days.

Benefits: Faster repair time, minimum down time, easier scheduling, increased sales, productive payroll expense. Customer site inventory is a turnkey system involving little involvement by customer. No hassle buying.

As program takes hold, we can expect to include drive line and brake product lines.

Worksheet 11

Tactics for
Market Segment: _Large fleets - clutches_

Sales Tactics	Feedback Mechanisms
Awareness	
Direct mail piece and brochure	Response card and telemarketing
Open house - show computer system	follow-up
and inventory availability	
Comprehension	
Personal selling	Direct customer feedback
Salesperson	
President	
Conviction	
Personal Selling	Direct customer feedback
Salesperson	
President	
Order	
Personal selling	Direct customer feedback
Salesperson	Semi-annual questionnaire
President	
Reorders	
Telemarketing	Appreciation meetings
	Focus Group: 1–2 per year

Worksheet 12

Budget Planning Worksheet for Market Segment: _Large fleets - clutches_

Expense	Mo. 1	Mo. 2	Mo. 3	Mo. 4	Mo. 5	Mo. 6	Mo. 7	Mo. 8	Mo. 9	Mo. 10	Mo. 11	Mo. 12	Annual Total
Brochure	500												500
Direct Mail	100												100
Open House	300												300
Computer Program	225												225
													$1,125

Worksheet 13

Implementation Scheduling Worksheet for Market Segment: _Large fleets - clutches_

	Tactic	Mo. 1	Mo. 2	Mo. 3	Mo. 4	Mo. 5	Mo. 6	Mo. 7	Mo. 8	Mo. 9	Mo. 10	Mo. 11	Mo. 12
Ad Agency	Brochure	X											
Office Personnel	Direct Mail	X											
Office Personnel	Open House	X											
	Personal Selling – Salesperson	X	X	X	X	X	X	X	X	X	X	X	X
	Personal Selling – President	X	X	X	X	X							
General Manager	Computer Program Set-up	X											
Counter Salesperson	Telemarketing		X	X	X	X	X	X	X	X	X	X	X
Office Personnel	Computer Updates, Delivery and Billing		X	X	X	X	X	X	X	X	X	X	X

Afterword

We end with one more piece of work for you to do—*keep doing what you have done in this program.*

The marketing foundation you have established will serve you well. It is important to note, though, that what you have is a foundation. Marketing is an ongoing process in a constantly changing business environment. The marketplace is dynamic. As such, the dynamics of your marketing efforts must keep pace.

How do you keep pace? By building upon the foundation you have established. How do you build upon the foundation? By listening to and learning about your customers and by excellence in execution.

You built feedback mechanisms into your sales program. Listen to your customers, and use what they tell you. Incorporate the feedback they give you into your analyses. The effect of the feedback may be to confirm your original analysis and plan of action or it may change your thinking in any number of areas.

You may need to rethink:

- Segmentation
- Segment selections
- Critical linkages
- Critical impacts

- Customer needs and benefits sought
- Customer purchasing characteristics
- Points of differentiation
- Marketing strategy for a target market
- Sales tactics for a target market

Continue to learn as much as you can about your customers. Join and participate in your customers' industry or trade association. Learn about your customers' customers. Find out what types of business pressures affect your customers.

For example:

- Are inventory levels and control important to your customer?
- Is quality control an issue for your customer?
- Do government regulations impact your customer?
- How cash flow sensitive is your customer?
- Is your customer in a seasonal business?

As we have discussed, the more you know about your customers, the more value you can create for them. By understanding their business, you can structure your products and services to help them deal with the issues affecting their success or failure. That has real value.

To conclude this program, look at the diagram depicting the Marketing Feedback Process. The steps in the process are marketing activities. Good marketing activities occur in a perpetual loop. As a company, you analyze the entire marketplace. You select target market segments you want to pursue. You analyze the segments and develop sales programs designed to capture business. You carry out the programs. During the process, you are receiving feedback from customers via dialogue with them. You incorporate that feedback, and start the loop again.

The Marketing Feedback Process

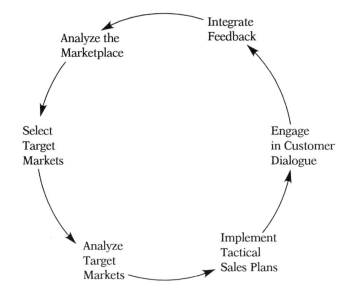

It is dialogue that enables you to learn about your customers and yourself. Your learning includes what is important to them and how well you are doing in satisfying them.

This repetitive looping of marketing activities that incorporates customer feedback and excellence in execution is the key to separating yourself from the crowd. This is the essence of achieving consistently good performance. That is what business is all about—good customers, good performance, and good profits.

Appendix

Reference Sources

To help with your research, you may want to use some of the reference sources listed below. The sources can provide you information for your segmentation studies and information on your markets. Most of the sources are available through the library.

Fairchild Fact Files
Provides sales, market trend, and buying habit information for product categories.

Encyclopedia of Associations
Provides details on over 19,500 national associations.

Trade Shows and Professional Exhibits Directory
Provides information on conferences, conventions, trade and industrial shows, merchandise marts, and expositions.

Trade Journal Directories

The following are sources you can consult to identify and locate trade journals for virtually any industry.

- *Ulrich's International Periodicals Directory*
- *Standard Rate and Data Service—Business Publications Rates and Data*
- *Bacon's Publicity Checker*
- *Writer's Market*
- *IMS/Ayer Directory of Publications*
- *Gale Directory of Publications*

U.S. Industrial Outlook
This federal government publication contains information and projections for 350 industries.

Standard and Poor's Industry Surveys
This source examines industries and their environment, including trends and problems.

Duns *Million Dollar Directory* and *Middle Market Directory*
Directories provide a listing of businesses $.5 million in net worth and larger. Available through Dun and Bradstreet. Contact Duns Marketing Service if local to you, or Dun and Bradstreet in New York City.

U.S. Department of Commerce

For data on consumers, businesses, and virtually anything else you can think of, the source with the most information is the U.S. Department of Commerce.

Included in their publications are:

- Census of the population
- Economic censuses
- Census of housing
- County business patterns
- Census tract reports
- Survey of current business

To help in determining what these publications offer, get a copy of *Measuring Markets: A Guide to the Use of Federal and State Statistical Data.* This guide tells you the type of information available, and where to send for it.

The Department of Commerce has field offices in many major cities in the United States.

State Department of Commerce

To get more regional or local information, contact your state's Department of Commerce. The types and volume of information available varies from state to state, but they should be a source for some good data.

Notes

1. Bonoma, Thomas. *The Marketing Edge* (New York, N.Y.: The Free Press, 1985).

2. McKenna, Regis. "Marketing Is Everything" (*Harvard Business Review,* Jan.–Feb., 1991) p. 70.

3. Kotler, Philip. *Marketing Management—Analysis, Planning, Implementation, Control* (Englewood Cliffs, N.J.: Prentice-Hall, 1988) p. 287.

4. Bonoma, Thomas and Benson Shapiro. *Segmenting the Industrial Market* (Lexington, Mass.: Lexington Books, 1983).

5. Primozic, Kenneth, Edward Primozic, and Joe Leben. *Strategic Choices* (New York, N.Y.: McGraw-Hill, Inc., 1991).

6. Ibid.

7. Berry, Leonard, Valarie Zeithaml, and A. Parasuraman. "Five Imperatives for Improving Service Quality" (*Sloan Management Review,* Summer, 1990) p. 35.

8. Porter, Michael. *Competitive Advantage* (New York, N.Y.: The Free Press, 1985) p. 3.

9. Ries, Al and Jack Trout. *Marketing Warfare* (New York, N.Y.: McGraw-Hill, Inc., 1986).

10. Ibid.

11. Ibid.

12. Ibid.

13. Ibid.

14. Ibid.

15. McKenna, Regis, *op. cit.* p. 75.

16. Kotler, Philip, *op. cit.* p. 595–596.

17. Ibid. p. 591–615.

18. Bonoma, Thomas. *The Marketing Edge* (New York, N.Y.: The Free Press, 1985).

19. Ibid.

20. Ibid.

21. Ibid.

Select Bibliography

Berry, Leonard, Valarie Zeitbaml, and A. Parasuraman. "Five Imperatives for Improving Service Quality", (*Sloan Management Review*, Summer, 1990).

Bonoma, Thomas. *The Marketing Edge* (New York, N.Y.: The Free Press, 1985).

Bonoma, Thomas and Benson Shapiro. *Segmenting the Industrial Market* (Lexington, Mass.: Lexington Books, 1983).

Breen, George Edward. *Do-It-Yourself Marketing Research* (New York, N.Y.: McGraw-Hill, 1977).

Buzzell, Robert and Bradley Gale. *The PIMS* Principles* (New York, N.Y.: The Free Press, 1987).

Kotler, Philip. *Marketing Management—Analysis, Planning, Implementation, Control* (Englewood Cliffs, N.J.: Prentice-Hall, 1988).

McKenna, Regis. "Marketing Is Everything" (*Harvard Business Review,* Jan.–Feb., 1991).

Peters, Thomas and Robert Waterman. *In Search of Excellence* (New York, N.Y.: Harper & Row, 1982).

Porter, Michael. *Competitive Strategy* (New York, N.Y.: The Free Press, 1980).

Porter, Michael. *Competitive Advantage* (New York, N.Y.: The Free Press, 1985).

Primozic, Kenneth, Edward Primozic, and Joe Leben. *Strategic Choices* (New York, N.Y.: McGraw-Hill, Inc., 1991).

Rapp, Stan and Tom Collins. *The Great Marketing Turnaround* (Englewood Cliffs, N.J.: Prentice-Hall, 1990).

Ries, Al and Jack Trout. *Positioning* (New York, N.Y.: McGraw-Hill, 1986).

Ries, Al and Jack Trout. *Marketing Warfare* (New York, N.Y.: Plume Books, 1986).

Sewell, Carl with Paul Brown. *Customers for Life* (New York, N.Y.: Doubleday Currency, 1990).

Sun Tzu. *The Art of War* (New York, N.Y.: Oxford University Press, 1963).

Thompson, Arthur and A. J. Strickland. *Strategy Formulation and Implementation* (Dallas, Texas: Business Publications, Inc., 1986).

Glossary

Advertising: Any paid form of non-personal communication or presentation of a product, service, idea, or company.

Alliances: A cooperative arrangement between two or more firms or individuals. Generally, the aligning parties complement each other for their mutual benefit.

Appreciation meeting: A gathering or meeting, normally social in nature, where a company expresses thanks to its customers for their loyalty and business.

Awareness: In the marketing and sales context, a step in the sales process. It indicates the level of understanding of a customer about your products, services, or company. The customer is aware of you, but does not fully understand what you do.

Breakeven analysis: The analysis of a product or service to determine the sales level required to cover fixed costs of providing that product or service.

Breakeven point: The specific sales level required to cover the fixed costs of providing a product or service.

Budget: The detailed financial component of a plan that guides the allocation of resources. It also provides a means to measure deviation of actual from desired results so corrective action can be taken.

Buying patterns: The collective variables customers consider when buying a product or service. Typical variables in a pattern are the frequency of purchases, quantity of purchases, and timing of purchases. The needs of the customer dictate what their buying pattern will be.

Cash flow: The movement of cash into and out of a business. When the receipt of monies exceeds the disbursement of monies over a specific time period, cash flow is positive. There is net cash available to the business. When disbursements exceed receipts, cash flow is negative. The business requires additional cash investment.

Cash flow statement: A financial document indicating the cash position of a business over a specified period of time.

Catalogs: A marketing tool for presenting products and services to customers. Catalogs are normally distributed through the mail and include descriptions of the products and services the company offers.

Channel of distribution: A pathway populated by parties that perform the marketing and sales tasks necessary to connect the manufacturer of a product with the end user.

Company strength: An asset of a company that potentially could provide it a competitive advantage.

Company weakness: A shortcoming of a company that potentially could place it at a competitive disadvantage.

Competitive move: An action taken by a competitor that could impact the success or failure of a company.

Competitor strength: An asset of a competitor that potentially could provide it a competitive advantage.

Competitor weakness: A shortcoming of a competitor that potentially could place it at a competitive disadvantage.

Comprehension: In the marketing and sales context, a step in the sales process. It indicates the level of understanding of a customer about your products, services, or company. The customer understands what you do but is not committed to buying from you.

Conviction: In the marketing and sales context, a step in the sales process. It indicates the level of understanding of a customer about your products, services, or company. The customer understands what you do and is developing a commitment to buy from you.

Coupons: A sales tactic used to entice customers to make buying decisions. Coupons usually take the form of a discounted price or increased value on a specific product or service. Customers generally must redeem the coupon in a specific time frame. The terms of the coupon are set by the seller.

Critical impact: A description of a specific aspect of a relationship between a company and its customer. The impact describes the effect a company has on its customer due to its performance or nonperformance. From the customer's perspective, the impact describes the benefits that will be received if the supplier performs.

Critical linkage: A description of a specific aspect of a relationship between a company and its customer. The linkage is a requirement a customer has of a company if it is to do business with them. From the customer's perspective, the linkage describes a need that must be fulfilled.

Customer: Actual or prospective purchaser of a product or service.

Customer audit: In the marketing and sales context, a method for determining the customer's perception of a company's performance. Via face to face, telephone, or mail, a company will question a customer on various aspects of its performance.

Customer benefit: The value provided to a customer from a product or service.

Customer feedback: Compliments, criticisms, or general information provided to a company by its customers about products, services, or any other aspect of their business. Generally, the feedback will show levels of satisfaction or dissatisfaction on the part of the customer.

Customer need: A want or desire on the part of the customer. These needs are the driving forces that underlie customers' actions and buying decisions.

Customer perspective: A look at a situation from the viewpoint of the customer.

Defensive strategy: An overall marketing and positioning strategy employed by the number one firm in a particular industry or market. The core of the strategy is to attack yourself and counter competitive moves.

Demographic segmentation: A technique that uses demographic information to segment customers.

Differentiation: Establishing a distinction in the mind of the customer about products, services, or a company.

Direct mail: A sales tactic for informing customers about your products, services, or company via information forwarded through the mail.

Direct response: A mechanism to give customers the opportunity to immediately respond to a company. Response is usually by telephone or mail directly to the company rather than through a retailer or other distribution channel.

Feedback mechanisms: Methods a company supplies to its customers for providing feedback on products, services, performance, or any other aspect of the company.

Flanking strategy: An overall marketing and positioning strategy usually employed by second tier companies in a market. The core of the strategy is the application of innovative thinking to capture market share.

Focus group: A simultaneous interview of a selected group of customers.

Geographic segmentation: A technique for segmenting customers based on where they are located.

Guerrilla strategy: An overall marketing and positioning strategy usually employed by the small companies in a market. The core of the strategy is to identify and exploit a very defined niche in a market.

Implementation plan: A specific action plan in which a series of tactics are used to meet objectives. The plan accounts for resource considerations and existing constraints.

Industry: A set of companies who have a commonality of products or services.

Industry association: An organization that analyzes and records data, trends, and issues impacting a specific industry.

Industry growth rate: The rate at which an industry is expanding, usually measured in sales dollars and/or percentage of growth.

Lost order analysis: A process for reviewing why an order was not obtained from a customer.

Market growth rate: The rate at which a specific market is expanding, usually measured in overall expenditures by customers.

Market research: Data pertaining to customers within a market segment.

Market research firm: An organization specializing in the gathering and analysis of market research data.

Market segment: A group of customers related by some common characteristic(s).

Market share: The portion of a market's total sales dollars secured by a particular firm, usually defined as a percentage of the total sales dollars.

Marketing: The process of planning and defining strategies and tactics for distribution of goods and services to users that creates value for the user and is profitable for the firm.

Marketing consultant: An individual or company who by training and/or experience is qualified to help a company with its marketing efforts.

Marketing innovation: The ability to create something new, be it product, service, or approach to the market.

Marketing plan: A written document defining a company's marketing strategy, including tactics, implementation plan, budget, and supporting financial statements.

Marketing strategy: The overall approach a firm takes in securing a position in a market.

News release: An announcement made by a firm and released to the media for distribution.

Niche market: A particular segment of a market that is of sufficient size to be profitable to a company, yet not large enough to attract the interest of major competitors.

Offensive strategy: An overall marketing and positioning strategy employed by the number two or three positioned forms in a particular industry or market. The core of the strategy is to attack a weakness in the number one firm's position.

Open house: A sales tactic whereby a company will invite customers and prospects to view their facility, products, and services.

Order: The point where a customer agrees to exchange money for goods or services provided by a company.

Personal selling: The sales tactic where direct contact between the customer and a company representative takes place for the purpose of getting a sale.

Point of purchase: The location where a customer deals with a company and purchases their products or services.

Point of sale: The location where a company deals with a customer and sells the products or services.

Point of sale differentiation: A tactic by which the company uses the point of sale to create a unique position for themselves in the customer's mind.

Price differentiation: A tactic by which the company uses price to create a unique position for themselves in the customer's mind.

Product: The tangible offerings a company provides to customers.

Product adaptation: The alteration or changing of a product or service to more closely meet the needs of the customer.

Product differentiation: A tactic by which the company uses the characteristics and capabilities of their product to create a unique position for themselves in the customer's mind.

Product mix: The array of products a company offers to customers. Also, how those products are combined to meet the needs of customers.

Profit and loss statement: The financial statement that shows the profit and/or loss of a company over a specified time period.

Prospects: Identified consumers, be they individuals or companies, who show good potential for buying a company's products or services.

Psychographic segmentation: A technique for segmenting customers that uses information relating to the psychology of the customer. Examples would include the customer's social class or lifestyle.

Publicity: A sales tactic using non-paid communication of a company's product or service, usually through some form of media.

Purchase characteristic: An attribute of customers that helps define their buying behavior.

Qualitative goals: Company goals that are defined in terms relating to work conditions, employees, community, or other non-financial and non-statistical areas.

Quantitative goals: Company goals that are defined in financial or statistical terms.

Rebates: A sales tactic that returns a portion of the purchase price in cash to the buyer from the seller.

Sales channel: An individual, agency, or company that functions as a selling entity.

Sales forecast: An estimate of future sales volume for a specified time period based on historical knowledge and market research data.

Sales message: The ideas, concepts, and points a company conveys to its customers via various selling methods.

Sales plan: The definable steps a company takes to secure sales.

Sales process: The movement of customers through a series of steps to secure orders.

Sales tactics: Tools companies use to convey their sales message, move customers through the sales process, and secure orders.

Segmenting techniques: Methods for identifying groups of customers who share common characteristics.

Seminar: An instructional and informational meeting.

Service differentiation: A technique by which the company uses the characteristics and capabilities of its services to create a unique position for themselves in the customer's mind.

Services: The intangible offerings a company provides to customers.

Singular attack: A focused approach to a competitive situation. The focus is on a single point or position of the competitor.

Support systems: The people and information technologies a company puts in place to support their overall operation.

Suspects: Identified consumers, be they individuals or companies, who show good potential for buying a company's products or services.

Target market: An identified market segment upon which a company focuses its resources and efforts in order to secure customers.

Target marketing: The process of segmenting a market, evaluating the segments, and identifying segments a company wishes to pursue.

Telemarketing: A sales tactic using the telephone to gather information and secure orders.

Trade journal/publication: A magazine or other printed media presenting information about a specific industry. An industry association or other objective third party is usually the source and publisher of this material.

Trade show: A convention type meeting where firms in a particular industry or related industries gather to display products and provide information to customers.

User group: A group of customers who purchase the same product or service. They meet to share information, and, where appropriate, supply information to and lobby suppliers.

Value: The inherent worth of a good or service.

Vertical industry: A group of customers related by the business they are in, often a starting point for market segmentation.

Worksheets

Foundation Packet
Worksheet A

Company Profile

Goals/Objectives
Qualitative

_____
_____
_____
_____

Quantitative

_____
_____
_____
_____

Business Characteristics
Products Description

_____
_____
_____

Services Description

_____
_____
_____

Customer Segments Served

_____
_____
_____

Worksheet B

Business Characteristics (cont.)

Location(s)

_____

_____

Geographic Area Served

_____

_____

Sales Channels

_____

_____

Resources Available for Marketing

| | *Time* | |
Name	*Hours*	*%*

Company strengths/areas of expertise

_____

_____

Company weaknesses/lack of expertise

_____

_____

Worksheet C

Analysis of Products and Services

Product Analysis

Description   Benefit

_____   _____

_____   _____

_____   _____

_____   _____

_____   _____

_____   _____

_____   _____

_____   _____

_____   _____

Services Analysis

Description   Benefit

_____   _____

_____   _____

_____   _____

_____   _____

_____   _____

_____   _____

_____   _____

_____   _____

_____   _____

Worksheet D

Business Analysis
for Competitor: _____

Location(s):   _____
                    _____
                    _____

Products offered: _____
                    _____
                    _____

Services offered: _____
                    _____
                    _____

Markets served: _____
                    _____
                    _____

Points of Sale: _____
(Channels)   _____
                    _____

Strengths: _____
                    _____
                    _____

Weaknesses: _____
                    _____
                    _____

Target Market Packet
Worksheet 1

**Overview for
Market Segment:** _____

Description

_____
_____
_____
_____
_____
_____
_____
_____
_____

\# Potential customers in segment: _____

Total sales in segment: Last year $ _____

                                 2 yrs. ago $ _____

                                 3 yrs. ago $ _____

Geographic dispersion

_____
_____
_____
_____
_____
_____

                               Date: _____

Worksheet 2

Customer Profile for
Market Segment: _____

Critical Linkages

CL #1 _____

  (N,B)* _____

_____

CL #2 _____

  (N,B) _____

_____

CL #3_____

  (N,B) _____

_____

CL #4 _____

CL #5 _____

CL #6 _____

Critical Impacts

CI #1 _____

  (N,B) _____

_____

CI #2 _____

  (N,B) _____

_____

CI #3 _____

  (N,B) _____

_____

N,B: Needs and/or Benefits Sought

Date: _____

Worksheet 2A

Initial Screening Questions
for Market Segment: _____

	Yes	No
Can my company currently satisfy the customer's linkage priorities?		
Can my company currently satisfy the customer's impact priorities?		
Can my company currently satisfy the customer's needs and benefits sought?		
Can I modify products, services, or my organization to satisfy needs?		
Can I use an alliance to bridge the gap between my capabilities and the customer's needs?		

Eliminate Segment

Date: _____

Worksheet 3

**Customer Profile—
Purchasing Characteristics
for Market Segment:** _____

Point(s) of Awareness (Q1) _____

_____

Pre-sale Requirements (Q2) _____

_____

Purchase Criteria (Q3,4,5,6) _____

_____

Sales Cycle (Q7) _____

Price Point (Q8) _____

Method of Payment (Q9) _____

Frequency of Purchase (Q10,11) _____

Product Mix (Q12,13) _____

_____

Point of Purchase (Q14) _____

Competition (Q15,16) _____

Post-sale Requirements (Q17,18,19) _____

Date: _____

Worksheet 4

Company Capabilities
for Market Segment: _____

My Company's Market Share _____ %

Ability to satisfy critical linkages   *Opportunity to differentiate?*

CL #1 _____   _____
(N,B) _____
_____

CL #2 _____   _____
(N,B) _____
_____

CL #3 _____   _____
(N,B) _____
_____

CL #4 _____   _____
CL #5 _____   _____
CL #6 _____   _____

Ability to satisfy critical impacts

CI #1 _____   _____
(N,B) _____
_____

CI #2 _____   _____
(N,B) _____
_____

CI #3 _____   _____
(N,B) _____
_____

N,B: Needs and/or Benefits Sought

Date: _____

Worksheet 5

**My Company's Capabilities
to Meet the Purchasing
Characteristics for
Market Segment:** _____

Point(s) of Awareness (Q1) _____

_____

Pre-sale Requirements (Q2) _____

_____

Purchase Criteria (Q3,4,5,6) _____

_____

_____

_____

_____

Sales Cycle (Q7) _____

Price Point (Q8) _____

Method of Payment (Q9) _____

Frequency of Purchase (Q10,11) _____

Product Mix (Q12,13) _____

_____

Point of Purchase (Q14) _____

Competition (Q15,16) _____

Post-sale Requirements (Q17,18,19) _____

Date: _____

Worksheet 6

Competitor Capabilities
for Market Segment: _____

Competitor: _____ Market Share _____ %

Ability to satisfy critical linkages   *Points of*
                                                                          differentiation?

CL #1 _____   _____
(N,B) _____
_____

CL #2 _____   _____
(N,B) _____
_____

CL #3 _____   _____
(N,B) _____
_____

CL #4 _____   _____
CL #5 _____   _____
CL #6 _____   _____

Ability to satisfy critical impacts

CI #1 _____   _____
(N,B) _____
_____

CI #2 _____   _____
(N,B) _____
_____

CI #3 _____   _____
(N,B) _____
_____

N,B: Needs and/or Benefits Sought

Date: _____

Worksheet 7

Competitor _____

Capabilities to Meet Purchasing

Characteristics for Market Segment: _____

Point(s) of Awareness (Q1) _____

_____

Pre-sale Requirements (Q2) _____

_____

Purchase Criteria (Q3,4,5,6) _____

_____

_____

_____

_____

Sales Cycle (Q7) _____

Price Point (Q8) _____

Method of Payment (Q9) _____

Frequency of Purchase (Q10,11) _____

Product Mix (Q12,13) _____

_____

Point of Purchase (Q14) _____

Competition (Q15,16) _____

Post-sale Requirements (Q17,18,19) _____

Date: _____

Worksheet 8

Final Screening Questions
for Market Segment: _____

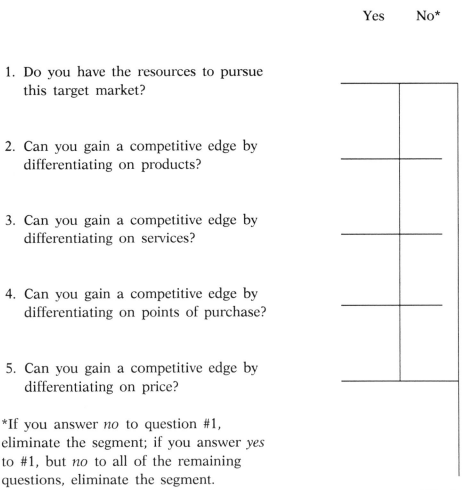

Yes   No*

1. Do you have the resources to pursue this target market?

2. Can you gain a competitive edge by differentiating on products?

3. Can you gain a competitive edge by differentiating on services?

4. Can you gain a competitive edge by differentiating on points of purchase?

5. Can you gain a competitive edge by differentiating on price?

*If you answer *no* to question #1, eliminate the segment; if you answer *yes* to #1, but *no* to all of the remaining questions, eliminate the segment.

Eliminate
Segment

Worksheet 9

Final Rating for
Market Segment: _____

How good can I be?

    Ability to meet needs (1–10):   _____

    Ability to differentiate:

        Rank from 1 to 4:   _____ Products

                                 _____ Services

                                 _____ Points of purchase

                                 _____ Price

What can I get out of it?

    Sales Forecasts   Best   _____ per _____

                                 Likely _____ per _____

                                 Worst _____ per _____

Overall rating for target market (A, B, or C): _____

Worksheet 10

Strategy for
Market Segment: _____

Market Strategy (choose one):

    Defensive (#1):   _____

    Offensive (#2, #3):   _____

    Flanking (#3–5, with resources):   _____

    Guerrilla (small player):   _____

Market Message:

_____

_____

_____

_____

_____

_____

_____

_____

_____

_____

_____

_____

_____

_____

_____

_____

_____

Worksheet 11

Tactics for
Market Segment: _____

Sales Tactics   **Feedback Mechanisms**

Awareness

_____   _____
_____   _____
_____   _____
_____   _____

Comprehension

_____   _____
_____   _____
_____   _____
_____   _____

Conviction

_____   _____
_____   _____
_____   _____
_____   _____

Order

_____   _____
_____   _____
_____   _____
_____   _____

Reorders

_____   _____
_____   _____
_____   _____
_____   _____

Worksheet 12

Expense	Mo. 1	Mo. 2	Mo. 3	Mo. 4	Mo. 5	Mo. 6	Mo. 7	Mo. 8	Mo. 9	Mo. 10	Mo. 11	Mo. 12	Annual Total

Budget Planning Worksheet for Market Segment: _____

Worksheet 13

Implementation Scheduling Worksheet for Market Segment: _____

Tactic	Mo. 1	Mo. 2	Mo. 3	Mo. 4	Mo. 5	Mo. 6	Mo. 7	Mo. 8	Mo. 9	Mo. 10	Mo. 11	Mo. 12

Market Research Tools
Critical Linkages Analysis

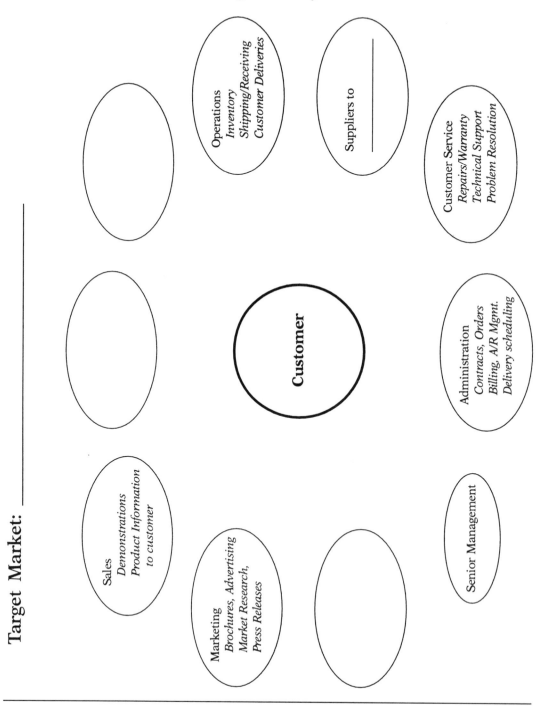

Target Market: _____

Critical Linkages Analysis

Target Market: _____

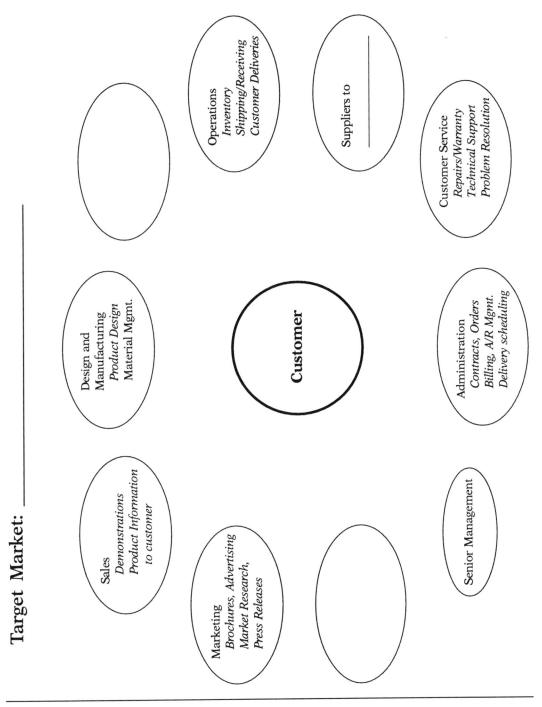

Operations
Inventory
Shipping/Receiving
Customer Deliveries

Suppliers to
_____

Customer Service
Repairs/Warranty
Technical Support
Problem Resolution

Design and
Manufacturing
Product Design
Material Mgmt.

Customer

Administration
Contracts, Orders
Billing, A/R Mgmt.
Delivery scheduling

Sales
Demonstrations
Product Information
to customer

Marketing
Brochures, Advertising
Market Research,
Press Releases

Senior Management

Critical Linkages Analysis

Target Market: _____

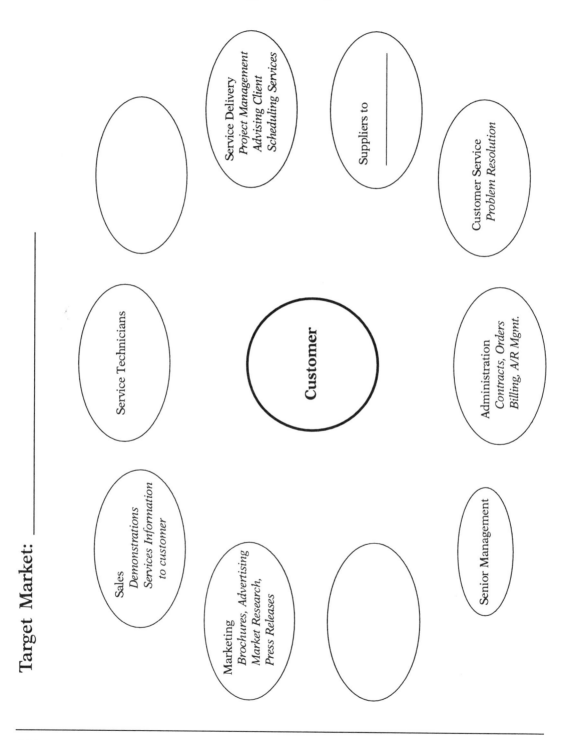

Customer

Service Delivery
Project Management
Advising Client
Scheduling Services

Suppliers to
_____

Customer Service
Problem Resolution

Service Technicians

Administration
Contracts, Orders
Billing, A/R Mgmt.

Sales
Demonstrations
Services Information
to customer

Marketing
Brochures, Advertising
Market Research,
Press Releases

Senior Management

Critical Linkages Analysis

Analysis Questions

Why is linkage #1 important to your organization?

_____

_____

How does this linkage benefit your business?

_____

_____

Are there any ways you would change the nature of this linkage?

_____

_____

Why is linkage #2 important to your organization?

_____

_____

How does this linkage benefit your business?

_____

_____

Are there any ways you would change the nature of this linkage?

_____

_____

Critical Linkages Analysis

(cont.)

Why is linkage #3 important to your organization?

_____

_____

How does this linkage benefit your business?

_____

_____

Are there any ways you would change the nature of this linkage?

_____

_____

Critical Linkages Analysis

Analysis Questions

Why is linkage #1 important to your organization?

_____

_____

How does this linkage benefit your business?

_____

_____

Are there any ways you would change the nature of this linkage?

_____

_____

Why is linkage #2 important to your organization?

_____

_____

How does this linkage benefit your business?

_____

_____

Are there any ways you would change the nature of this linkage?

_____

_____

Critical Linkages Analysis

(cont.)

Why is linkage #3 important to your organization?

_____

_____

How does this linkage benefit your business?

_____

_____

Are there any ways you would change the nature of this linkage?

_____

_____

Critical Impacts Analysis

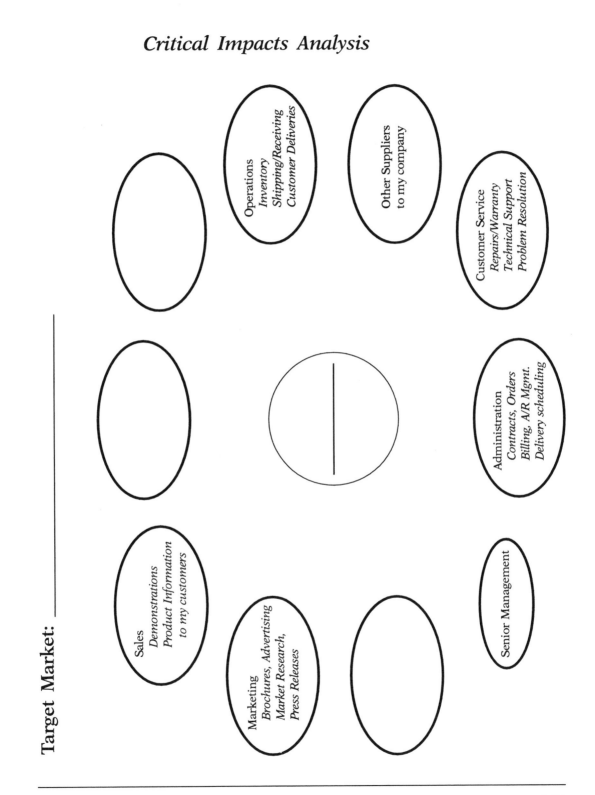

Target Market: _____

Operations
Inventory
Shipping/Receiving
Customer Deliveries

Other Suppliers
to my company

Customer Service
Repairs/Warranty
Technical Support
Problem Resolution

Administration
Contracts, Orders
Billing, A/R Mgmt.
Delivery scheduling

Senior Management

Sales
Demonstrations
Product Information
to my customers

Marketing
Brochures, Advertising
Market Research,
Press Releases

Critical Impacts Analysis

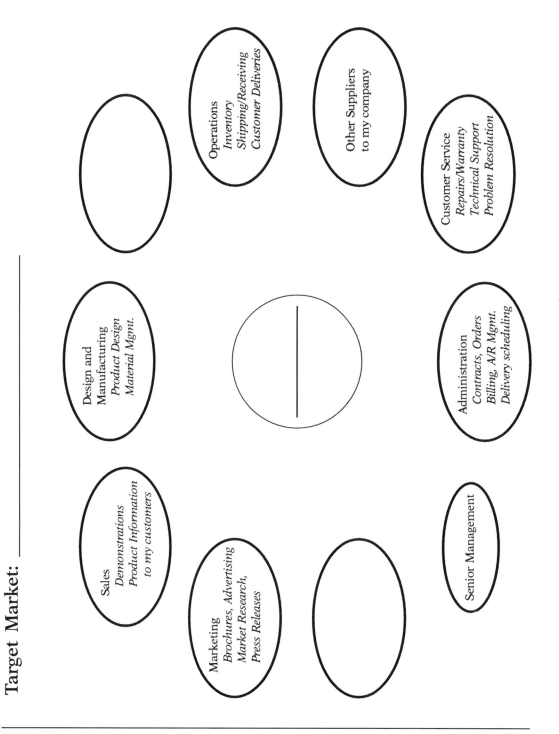

Target Market: _____

Operations
Inventory
Shipping/Receiving
Customer Deliveries

Other Suppliers
to my company

Customer Service
Repairs/Warranty
Technical Support
Problem Resolution

Design and
Manufacturing
Product Design
Material Mgmt.

Administration
Contracts, Orders
Billing, A/R Mgmt.
Delivery scheduling

Sales
Demonstrations
Product Information
to my customers

Marketing
Brochures, Advertising
Market Research,
Press Releases

Senior Management

Critical Impacts Analysis

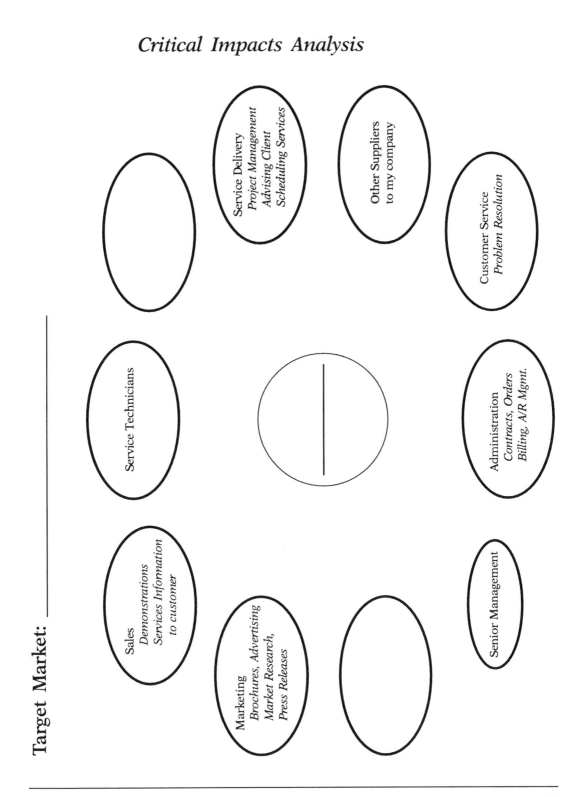

Target Market: _____

- Service Delivery
  *Project Management
  Advising Client
  Scheduling Services*
- Other Suppliers
  to my company
- Customer Service
  Problem Resolution
- Service Technicians
- Administration
  *Contracts, Orders
  Billing, A/R Mgmt.*
- Sales
  *Demonstrations
  Services Information
  to customer*
- Marketing
  *Brochures, Advertising
  Market Research,
  Press Releases*
- Senior Management

Critical Impacts Analysis

Analysis Questions

How does the #1 impact area affect your company?

_____

_____

Why is this so?

_____

_____

If you could alter the impact, what changes would you make?

_____

_____

How does the #2 impact area affect your company?

_____

_____

Why is this so?

_____

_____

If you could alter the impact, what changes would you make?

_____

_____

Critical Impacts Analysis

(cont.)

How does the #3 impact area affect your company?

_____

_____

Why is this so?

_____

_____

If you could alter the impact, what changes would you make?

_____

_____

Purchase Characteristics Questionnaire for Products

We need your assistance. We are working to improve our products and services to you. We want to ask you some questions about _____ products.

It will take about 5 minutes of your time. Will you help us?

Thank you very, very much!

Please answer the following questions while thinking about the last time you bought _____ .

1. Where did you first hear about or see this product?

   - Advertising
   - Radio
   - TV
   - Magazine

   - Mailer
   - Newspaper
   - Telephone sales

   - Referral (friend)
   - Catalog
   - Other (Specify): _____

2. When thinking about selecting this product, where do you get information to help you make this selection?

   - Advertising
   - Radio
   - TV
   - Magazine
   - Newspaper

   - Mailer
   - Other
   - Telephone sales
   - Catalog
   - In Store

   - From Salesperson
   - Friend
   - Other (specify): _____

3. When buying this product, what feature(s) do you look for? _____

   _____

4. When comparing similar products, what do you compare? _____

   _____

5. Are there any services that could help you make your purchase decision for this product?

- Information on (specify):
  _____
- Product demonstration
- Explain how it works
- Explain how I can install it

- Explain how I can use it
- Help me compare similar products
- Help me understand which product best suits my needs
- Referrals from other customers

6. Can you list at least five (5) criteria you use to decide to buy this product?

_____ 1. _____

_____ 2. _____

_____ 3. _____

_____ 4. _____

_____ 5. _____

Please rank these criteria in order of importance. (Use the short line next to each criteria above to indicate ranking from 1 to 5.)

7. How long a time is it from when you get interested in buying this product until you actually buy it? _____

8. When buying this product, what price range is right for you?

From _____ to _____

9. How do you usually pay for this product?
- Cash
- Expect monthly billing
- Bank loan

- Visa
- MasterCard
- Discover

- American Express
- Store card
- Other

10. How many times do you buy this product?

_____ per week or _____ per month or _____ per year

11. How many more times will you buy this product?

_____ Next week or _____ next month or _____ next year

12. What other products do you buy with this one?

_____

_____

13. What other products would you like to buy with this one?

_____

_____

14. Where do you usually buy this product? (Check all that apply.)
   - Catalog
   - Food Store
   - Drug Store
   - Specialty Store
   - Department Store
   - Discount Store
   - Dealer
   - Other Store (specify): _____

15. When you think of this product, what brand comes to mind first?

_____

_____

16. When you think of buying this product, from where and whom do you first think to buy it?

_____

_____

17. What result or benefits do you expect from purchasing this product?

_____

_____

18. What services would you like after you buy this product?
    - Installation
    - Warranty
    - Instruction on: _____

    - Technical information on: _____

    _____

    Other:_____

    _____   _____

19. How much do you think would be reasonable to pay for these services?

_____

_____

20. What is your zip code? _____

Purchase Characteristics Questionnaire for Services

We need your assistance. We are working to improve our products and services to you. We want to ask you some questions about _____ services.

It will take about 5 minutes of your time. Will you help us?

Thank you very, very much!

Please answer the following questions while thinking about the last time you bought _____ .

1. Where did you first hear about or see this service?

   • Advertising   • Mailer   • Referral (friend)

   • Radio   • Newspaper   • Catalog

   • TV   • Telephone sales   • Other (Specify): _____

   • Magazine

2. When thinking about selecting a company to provide this service, where do you get information to help you make this selection? (Check all that apply.)

   • Advertising   • Mailer   • From Salesperson

   • Radio   • Other   • Friend

   • TV   • Telephone sales   • Other (specify): _____

   • Magazine   • Catalog

   • Newspaper   • In Store

3. When selecting a company to provide this service, what feature(s) do you look for? _____

   _____

---

4. When comparing companies offering similar services, what do you compare? _____

_____

5. Are there any factors that could help you make your purchase decision for this service?

- Information on (specify): _____
- Explain how it works
- Explain how I can use it

- Help me compare similar services
- Help me understand which service best suits my needs
- Referrals from other clients

6. Can you list at least three (3) criteria you use to decide to buy this service?

_____ 1. _____
_____ 2. _____
_____ 3. _____
_____ 4. _____
_____ 5. _____

Please rank these criteria in order of importance. (Use the short line next to each criteria above to indicate ranking from 1 to 5.)

7. How long a time is it from when you get interested in using this service until you actually use it? _____

8. When paying for this service, what price range is right for you?
From _____ to _____

9. How do you usually pay for this service?

- Cash
- Expect monthly billing
- Bank loan

- Visa
- MasterCard
- Discover

- American Express
- Store card
- Other _____

10. How many times do you use this service?

_____ per week or _____ per month or _____ per year

11. How many more times will you use this service?

_____ next week or _____ next month or _____ next year

12. Are there other services you usually receive with this one?

_____

_____

13. What other services would you like to receive with this one?

_____

_____

14. Where do you usually buy this service? (Check all that apply.)

- Specialists
- Dealer
- Other (specify): _____

15. When you think of this service, what company comes to mind first?

_____

_____

16. When you think of using this service, from where and whom do you first think to get it?

_____

_____

17. What result or benefits do you expect from using this service?

_____

_____

18. What other services would you like after you use this service?
    - Warranty
    - Instruction on: _____
    _____
    - Technical information on: _____
    _____
    - Other information on _____
    _____

19. How much do you think would be reasonable to pay for these services?

_____

_____

20. What is your zip code? _____

Index

McKenna, Regis, 111, 112, 113

Niche, 79. *See* Market segment

Offensive marketing strategy, 76-77
  and sales plan development, 86-87
Orders, 81
  and reorders, creating, 90-91

Parasuraman, A., 111, 112
Personal selling, 83
Peters, Thomas, 113
Points of purchase, as segmenting
  technique, 6-7
Points of sale, differentiation by, 63-64
Porter, Michael, 112, 113
Price, differentiation by, 64-65
Primozic, Edward, 111, 113
Primozic, Kenneth, 111, 113
Product mix, as segmenting
  technique, 7
Products, differentiation by, 61-62
Products/services analysis, 42-43
Profit and loss (P&L) statement, 93, 97
Promotion, 83-84
Prospects, 80, 84
Publicity, 82
Purchase characteristics
  of customers, 13
  questionnaire, 16, 17-18

Qualifying market segments, 18-20
Qualitative goals, 40-41
Quantitative goals, 40

Rapp, Stan, 113
Reorders, 81
  creating, 90-91
Repeat customers, 80

Resource capabilities, 59-60
  budget requirements and, 92-93
  and defensive strategies, 77-78
  financial, 91-94
Retailers, 4-5
Revenues, 92-93
Ries, Al, 112
Risk, of flanking strategy, 78

Sales
  calculating, 46
  historical, 68
Sales forecast, 67-69
Salespeople, 68
Sales plans
  budgets and, 91-94
  developing, 3, 75-108, 84-99
  goals and, 85-87
  implementing, 97-99
  measurement of results and, 95-97
  tactics selection and, 88-91
  target market implementation plans
    and, 94-95
Sales process, 80-81
Sales promotion, 83-84
  plan components, 84, 85
Sales tactics, 81-84
Sales volume. *See* Sales forecast
Schedules, implementation of, 94-95
Screening process, and market
  segments, 19
Segmentation. *See* Market segmentation
Segmenting techniques, 8-9. *See also*
  Market segmentation
Selling, personal, 83
Services
  differentiation by, 62-63
  analysis of, 42-43
Sewell, Carl, 113
Shapiro, Benson, 111
Slogan, and defensive strategy, 77